My First Novel

tales of woe and glory

writers tribe books

Published by Writers Tribe Books
www.writerstribebooks.com

Compilation copyright © 2013 by Writers Tribe Books

My First Novel is an original publication of Writers Tribe Books. This work
has never before appeared in book form. Cheryl Strayed's essay, "On Torch"
originally appeared in the online blog *mjroseblog.typepad.com* on May 15,
2006. Rick Moody's essay first appeared as the introduction to his book,
Garden State, in non-annotated form.

Book cover design by Ryan Basile
Interior design by Amy Inouye

Published in the United States of America

ISBN 978-1-937746-15-5

Library of Congress Control Number: 2013942742

For information on L.A. Writers' Lab's writing workshops,
please go to <u>lawriterslab.com</u>

ACKNOWLEDGMENTS

A great many people have contributed to this book. Thank you to my assistant, Katharine Wilson, and our L.A. Writers' Lab intern, Sarah Long, for proofing and copy-editing the manuscript. A very special thank you to my dear friend, Leslie Schwartz, who opened her Rolodex and introduced me to many of the authors who contributed the work in these pages. It's so nice to have a writer friend with impeccable social skills. Thanks to Libby Flores at PEN Center USA for giving me the opportunity to teach The Mark Program, and to Adam Somers, Michelle Meyering, and all the staff at PEN Center USA for doing all that they do to benefit writers here in the U.S. and around the world. Thank you to my students at L.A. Writers' Lab for sharing your curiosity and passion with me.

And finally, my most heartfelt thank you to all of the authors who contributed their time and energy to this book. Without your candor and insight, this book would not exist.

TABLE OF CONTENTS

INTRODUCTION

Maybe it's because I'm the son of a shrink, but the creative process has always fascinated me more than the result. Of course, writers need a grounding in craft, but too often the creative process gets objectified. Words like *craft* or *technique* imply an "outside in" approach, where the author is expected to manufacture pages without having any skin in the game. To write well costs something. If the writer is good, he's not just exposing himself, but shedding something in order to get at a deeper truth. It is this aspect that most excites me about teaching writing: how to work with the channel, how to help the writer open up to the story that lives within.

There are many gifted writers who struggle, feel blocked, or have blind spots, and breaking through can be difficult. Our world has gotten so noisy that it's nearly impossible to turn off all the devices and get quiet. When Picasso put a bike seat and handlebars together and called it *Bull's Head*, it was the work of a focused subconscious unencumbered by Twitter. In fact, being an artist these days seems to be more about marketing than content. It seems that what we have to say is less important than whether or not we are making ourselves heard. Artists are not celebrated for their work, but for their sales. Maybe it's always been like this, but if the world is going to be changed through a shift in consciousness, it will almost certainly begin with artists. Art should not be considered the purview of a privileged few.

In 2012, I was invited to teach The Mark Program for PEN Center USA. It is a finishing school for a small group of authors who have completed PEN Center USA's Emerging Voices Fellowship and are now readying their work for publication. It was hard work, but I loved it.

What I've learned as a teacher is the necessity for validation. I'm not talking about handholding in lieu of criticism, but a deep, abiding curiosity in what the writer is attempting to express, *because it is always valid*. He might not understand it. The truth might lie beneath a hornet's nest of false starts, but ultimately it is there.

While teaching The Mark Program, with its goal of readying writers for publication, I began to sense an aspect of the process that needed addressing, something more ephemeral than craft. As an addendum to the workshop, I began to imagine a book where a group of published authors shared their experience of writing their first book. What did they really go through? What was their process? Real life accounts — no theorizing — with the goal of demystifying the experience, that weird transition when the publishing gods suddenly reach down and christen you a writer.

When I was twelve, I read James Michener's *The Drifters*, an eight-hundred page tome that I lost myself in for two weeks while traveling through Italy with my family. I was in awe of this dude who created this fictional world. How did he know so much? I wanted to sit down and have a root beer with him. (I was twelve.) I wanted to ask him how he persevered. Surely there was a moment when he thought to himself, "This is too difficult."

Samuel Beckett famously said, "I can't go on, I'll go on." If you are struggling, or wondering if you are a writer, I hope this book will help. When we make "getting published" the goal, we lose sight of the reason we write. It is a challenge to stay with the words when we're dreaming about the day we can quit our day job. This book hopefully illustrates how writers stay with the process without losing sight of the result. Inside are twenty-five accounts of writers' journeys in creating their first book — twenty-five separate road maps to the same destination.

I hope you find it useful.

AL WATT
Los Angeles, May 2013

PS: 100% of the net proceeds for this book are being donated to PEN Center USA's Emerging Voices Fellowship. To read more about PEN Center USA, or to make a donation, please go to penusa.org.

THE DRAWER

Aimee Bender

Every agent panel I ever attended dissed the short story collection. "It's not a good seller," they said. Or: "I rarely represent short stories." I sat in the audience with the other hopeful writers and felt bad; I was working on short stories and I liked reading short stories and felt I was learning something about the world of short stories and I gravitated toward the concise. At the time, I had no plans for a novel. What to do?

There weren't a whole lot of options.

Continue to work on short stories.

Years later, I had a full collection — one that felt done, and complete, and ready to find a place for itself. I had started a novel, but I did not know if I could pull it off. I had never written one before, and my writer's impulse was a short story one, which tended to push toward an end and finish under twenty pages. Sometimes eight pages. Sometimes two. I did not know if I could unravel this impulse enough to write anything substantially longer.

I met both my agent and editor around the same time. The editor was incredibly supportive but, as was the way of the industry, wanted to sign me up for a two-book deal, putting the novel first. A two-book deal! I was thrilled and stunned. Except . . . the novel wasn't done. It was about eighty pages so far and who knew if it would ever go anywhere. I knew I needed time to wander around with it and see what it might become.

This was the first big decision I made with my agent. I had a book of stories that felt ripe to me. I had a novel in progress. Publishing did not like to start with stories — a launch, they generally said, was better with a novel. But I couldn't imagine putting the stories in a drawer and adding that kind of pressure on the novel.

We discussed it at length and my agent was thoroughly on board. We agreed that the deal sounded wonderful, but only if the stories came out first.

This could have gone many ways, but my editor is open-minded and extremely encouraging, and he agreed.

As it turned out, the stories were ultimately a better "launch" for me than the novel. They were a better way for me to introduce myself. Also, this was 1998, and several women came out with story collections around then that had a magical/fairy tale feel to them. Judy Budnitz. Julia Slavin. Stacey Richter — who isn't as into the magical element but has such a strong and appealingly fresh voice. I was able to join this wave in a way I might not have.

The moral here isn't stick to your guns no matter what. It isn't "force the system to bend to you." It's just that what I had was stories. That's what I wrote; that's what I had. Ride the river you're on. For me, the moral is something like:

work with what you have, not what you might have, or what the market wants. If there's a book that feels ready, and it's tugging to leave the booknest, then push for it, or at least try.

What happens next is largely out of the writer's hands. But it's the writer's decision to put something in a drawer and it should always be the writer's decision. If a live creature of a book goes in a drawer due to marketplace concerns or practical advisement from others, that writer may lose interest in writing, and who could blame him? If he cannot get it published and makes that drawer decision on his own, then that is different. That's acceptance. To drawer something before giving it a go skips over any chance of acceptance. I later did put a novel in a drawer — not the one I'd started (which I ended up really enjoying writing), but the next one, one that just wasn't working, after trying and trying for years — but it was my decision and I found it both painful and relieving.

The drawer is perhaps as active a part of the writer's life as the non-drawer, the pages that see the light and go to people. In my view, it's important not to work on everything, to put things aside that aren't quite clicking, to admit that something is off, to fish around until the more vital writing kicks back in. Likewise, it's important not to take a wriggling, bursting poem or story and let it shrivel inside darkness.

Aimee Bender is the author of *The Girl in the Flammable Skirt* and *The Particular Sadness of Lemon Cake* among others and has a new collection of stories coming out in fall 2013. Her short fiction has been published in *Granta, Harper's, The Paris Review, Tin House* and more.

For more information, go to www.flammableskirt.com.

LABOR

Cynthia Bond

Fifteen years ago, I lived in an oven of a guesthouse in a forgotten enclave of Los Angeles known as Silverlake. Long before Intelligentsia turned coffee into gold nuggets; before actresses and writers posed in windows like cardboard props; before ten-dollar-a-stem florists and "hand-crafted cocktails" at Café Stella, I began working on my first novel.

In 1998, my neighborhood bodega sold sour pickles and canned molé on Sunset; a Panadería filled the air every morning with warm buttery cuernos, and a tattoo parlor buzzed pride into golden brown skin. I paid five hundred dollars a month for my one-bedroom, complete with a garden and a basement, where the previous tenant, a Santeria Priestess, had performed ceremonies and Orisha healings before she died. I found dozens of half-burned candles in the basement cupboards when I moved in. Men with lost eyes still wandered to the hidden back lot from time to time and tore off pieces of the bitter rue that had overtaken the yard. Crows congregated in the leaning palms and cawed and purred above my roof.

I had written short stories for years, the same characters

emerging again and again like ocean waves, then dispersing. At 984 Hyperion Avenue, they pushed into my dreams until one day, exhausted, I began gathering these disconnected stories. I rooted, searched and retrieved pages — some scrawled in notebooks, some written on loose typing paper, and others typed into a DOS windowless computer. I discarded many characters and journeys — countless seeds for other novels. Those that fit together, I stacked, then wrote the headings on Post-its. I made a clothes line and hung the yellow papers like tiny handkerchiefs in front of my desk. Over the next year I patched them together into a quilt and attempted the first draft of my novel.

There were problems. Flashbacks fed into flashbacks, which fed into more flashbacks. Descriptions flowered too sticky sweet and then wilted on the page, but I remembered reviews I'd received when my short story, *Ruby*, had been published in an anthology by Anchor Books. The newspapers and periodicals that said I was a "name to watch." The meticulous encouragement of teachers pushed me as well: playwright Jim Picket, novelist John Rechy and Terry Wolverton.

But it was home — the excruciating wonder and horror of my childhood that forced me, compelled me to finish my book. Working on my novel was a journey that started long before I wrote the first line.

Growing up as the child of a college English Professor played a vital part. At five, hearing my father quote Shylock's soliloquy from *The Merchant of Venice* while restringing his guitar. At eight, sitting on Maya Angelou's lap in our home on Oak Street and asking her, "Why *did* the caged bird sing?" Meeting Gwendolyn Brooks, Nikki Giovanni and others on the Kansas University campus where my father, one of the few black professors, hosted many of the famous writers and activists of the day. Listening to those voices speaking before hushed, expectant crowds helped me to know that truth could scent the air like honeysuckle, that it could be breathed in.

However it was my mother, and her hometown of Liberty Community, an all-black town in East Texas, that truly taught me the music of language.

A stunningly beautiful and quite accomplished woman today, my mother grew up in poverty on a small farm in the piney woods. She has a collection of small faded scars on her body. As children, my sister and I would point to one and ask her to tell that chapter of her life — being trapped in a freshly dug well filling with water; having children pick on her every day for having light skin and straight hair, until she learned to fight and win against boys and girls five times her size. We heard the vibrant stories of triumph and pain over and over like a well-worn favorite picture book.

We learned about our grandfather, a douser and carpenter, born in 1866, the son of a slave master and a slave. My mother was the seventieth and last of his children. As my sister and I grew older, we learned about my mother's sister who was murdered by the Klan. In many ways, this is how *Ruby* began. I grew up with this town, this time infused in my spirit.

During my childhood, I also lived with horrific abuse. These memories cut through me like shrapnel, and like my main character Ruby, I too wandered from place to place. Instead of the red clay roads of Liberty, I drove my yellow Ford Fiesta around Los Angeles, often in a daze. Pulling over to howl into the narrow hollow of my worn car. My relationship with my father was ripped into pieces. The guilt my mother felt was almost impossible to bear.

I began working with homeless youth living on the streets of Hollywood. There, I heard stories that mirrored my own, and others that haunted me at night. The teens who lived through violence and cult abuse. Police beating young people for living in squats or for having the audacity of being gender outlaws. I saw firsthand the lives of young prostitutes — those who had been forced into this horror as children, and those who fell into the quicksand of Santa Monica Blvd. as teens. I knew youth who survived, and those who did not.

As I wrote the first, second and third draft of *Ruby*, all of these people and places mixed and blended together. New characters entered into the story on their own volition, whispering, then shouting themselves into existence, so that this piece is both fact and fiction. However, the abuse that lives on the pages is pulled from life. Each atrocity is some part of a true experience.

Fourteen long years later, in August of 2012, I submitted the completed third draft of my novel to the agent I had been lucky enough to land. It had taken me four years to do the rewrite she had asked for, and then, once mailed, I waited eagerly, foolishly, for her to read it in a week. Instead, I waited six months.

In spite of all that I had lived through, this waiting was the hardest. In spite of her telling me, quite kindly, that four manuscripts had come in before mine. In spite of the fact that New York faced a hurricane and that the life of an agent is chock full of festivals and contracts and work, my rewrite went unread, or worse, I feared, had been read and inspired a deathly silence. A ghost-like rejection.

After the first month of waiting I took out a little teaspoon and began digging a shallow hole of doubt. The second month I burrowed deeper . . . past the thin, feather roots of hopeful grass. The third month I reached stone, smooth, dark and round. The fourth, I traded my silver spoon for a nearby shovel. I began digging in earnest.

I thought about the months, years of sitting on lightly padded leather, my neck tightening, the tears sliding, dripping from my chin when I entered the rooms my characters inhabited. The smoky lofts of 1950s Manhattan, where the Literati gathered, and the hidden houses in the South where little girls waited for grown men to enter. The money paid when they left. I lived through the cracking of souls like walnuts, through the loss of love. Lived through the joy as well, hands parting a curtain of insanity, breathing life into an empty chest. All of that, the reading, rereading, the sending off to be edited, the many, many years before, when I wore a gray shirt for two weeks, unable to dress, to eat, to speak, but I found my way to a writing class and wrote myself out of crazy. Wrote through my father's death. Wrote through illness, a stay in the hospital, and the destruction of two relationships. I wrote myself into a world of hope.

Years later, after being awarded the Emerging Voices PEN Fellowship, I suddenly had the freedom to write the second draft. I was eight months pregnant when the Fellowship began, and had my daughter, Malia, while completing the amazing curriculum. Finding time, wrestling against sleeplessness, nursing her, loving her beyond reason and then writing. Eyes on my screen for hours at Swork coffee house in Eagle Rock, the familiar ease of the staff, as if I were on the schedule with them.

I wrote in an old church office, typed unfettered evil onto my screen, let a pedophile, a sadist and a murderer enter my body each day to tell his side of the story — my commitment to give each character a voice, to suspend my judgment, to submit, for the good of the novel, my eyes, my mouth, my flesh to this man. I was a reporter, trying to get a Klansman to open up by nodding in seeming agreement. My only condition was that he could not enter my home, could not live beside my daughter — all else was allowed.

Finishing the Fellowship, and, through painstaking work, in 2008, winning Nicole Aragi, the agent of my dreams, who represented my favorite authors, Pulitzer Prize winner Junot Díaz, Edwidge Danticat, Jonathan Safran Foer. I had submitted a query letter. Next she allowed me to submit fifty pages, then the entire 900-page opus. Less than two weeks later she called to tell me that she wanted to represent me. I screamed when I got off the telephone — terrifying my daughter, crying, gulping in air on the bedroom floor. I had to explain to her that Mommy was happy. I traveled to New York to meet with Nicole and she gave me copious notes. Cut the prologue; break the manuscript into two or three books and much more.

Coming back to L.A. Going through divorce, foreclosure, a miscarriage and not being able to lift my fingers to the keyboard for two years. Then forming Blackbird Writing Collective and beginning again, parsing through her notes, page by page, restructuring the arc of the story, outline after outline, scenes written and rewritten and rewritten and then rewritten again. Finally at long last submitting what would be the first of three novels. Racing to get it to her before the August break — the month the publishing industry goes on hiatus.

Then beginning the interminable vigil. The fifth month of waiting I dug a grave for myself as a writer. All of my hope, faith and work laid to rest. What had I been imagining all of those years? Living as a writer, traveling with my daughter to readings, showing her how to succeed in the world, that her mama could build the life she wanted, which meant that she could as well.

Letting go of a dream is a death. It is submitting the resistant lump of certain knowledge. And what has been — clutching the reins of destiny too tight for angels to lend a hand, becomes slack. It is leaving the palms open, watching the horse trot away into the stars. It is surrendering thoughts held for over a decade. It is bending the head. Sitting on a girlfriend's back porch and looking towards the night sky, hearing the chimes sifting the wind twenty inches away. It is laying down all arms . . . all weapons . . . all arrows poised against the will of God if it does not match one's own.

I had reached an odd, silent peace as I watched a part of me cease to breathe. It was easy to let her die. It was a relief.

In that aftermath. Two days after giving up the ghost, the email from my agent came. The one apologizing for her absence, the one that said she had finished my third draft. The one that said she, "loved, loved, loved" my rewrite. That she had been, "consumed" by her and she was "sooooooo impressed," by all the work I had done.

She submitted my book on a Monday, on Tuesday there was an offer, a pre-empt from Hogarth Press, a division of Random House. An offer for both domestic and international rights that showed, on a balance sheet, their great and astounding confidence in my work.

By Thursday we had made a deal.

My novel will be published in May of 2014, with the promise of full PR regalia — book tours, press and perhaps my beloved NPR.

I now see that completing my novel was very much like the duplicity of labor. Like the glowing, saccharine face of the doula who taught a natural childbirth class I attended. The one who told a room-full of trusting pregnant women, upon feeling a contraction, to say "Wow" instead of "Ow." Like all of the mothers who watched my golden brown belly rising like baking bread and said nothing. No hint of what was to come.

Thirty-seven hours before my daughter's birth, I felt the first pain stabbing through my core. My husband and I urgently called the midwife. When she arrived, she smiled knowingly and told me that I had only dilated one centimeter.

She told me that labor had not actually begun.

I believe that writing a book is like that.

However, unlike the last hours of labor — writers have the ability to opt out. To decide that the pain is too much to bear to put their work into the world — to give birth. I did just that — for months, years at a time. But, like the doctor saying there is only one more push, when, in fact there were fifty, perhaps sixty more — the end result is the miracle of a child.

Now that I have sent my book into the world, I know that it was worth it.

A few nights ago, I had a dream about authors. I saw writer after writer standing in front of a flag saying the pledge of allegiance, like I was forced to do in grade school, hand on my heart. In my dream I looked and saw that the flags were made of pages. I woke up and realized in the quiet, enveloping dark, that this is what I had done when I had embarked upon this journey so long ago. I realize that this is what I must do, over and over, with each new book, each new sentence, to continue to see my work in the world.

Cynthia Bond is a writer and educator. An Emerging Voices Pen Fellow, Cynthia's writing has been critically praised and has appeared in various anthologies.

Cynthia has been working with at-risk youth for more than twelve years. She has collaborated with organizations including UCLA and the LA Cultural Affairs Dept., to create teen writing and photo exhibits which have been featured on MTV, in the *LA Weekly*, LA City Hall, multiple art gallery's and the National Drug Court Office in Washington D.C. Cynthia coordinated a writing/

performance workshop with comedian Ellen Degeneres, which focused on helping homeless youth in Hollywood write their truth.

Cynthia currently conducts Journaling and Therapeutic writing groups for Paradigm Malibu, an Adolescent Treatment Center. Through written expression, she assists teen rehab participants in gaining new perspectives on their lives and the recovery process.

She currently lives in Los Angeles with her eight-year-old daughter. Cynthia's first novel, *Ruby*, will be published in May of 2014 by Hogarth Press, a division of Random House.

For more information, go to www.cynthiabond.com.

THE BIRTH OF CHRISTOPHER

Allison Burnett

I spent my twenties as most young writers do: on my hands and knees, crawling through a self-made gauntlet of anxiety, embarrassment, shame, and despair. When people asked me what I did for a living, I found it hard to answer without swallowing hard and fighting back tears. I called myself a novelist, but the world knew me only as a legal proofreader. Five nights a week, from 11:30 p.m. until dawn, my youth and talent were squandered in a tiny beige room inside a vertical black coffin, poring over words I knew how to spell but whose meanings I only vaguely understood. (What the hell *is* a debenture, anyway?) As the sun rose, I'd gaze out my window at the other office towers of midtown Manhattan and think *I'll die here.*

In December 1984, I decided to challenge my destiny. I rented an apartment in Provincetown, Massachusetts, where I would write if not The Great American Novel, then *a* novel. It might not earn me enough money to lay down my proofer's pencil, but at least it would enable me to look people in the eye at dinner parties when they asked me what I did for a living. I chose Provincetown because I knew it was a snowy wasteland, populated mostly by gay men, which meant there would be no romantic or sexual distractions. Also, the apartment came without a telephone or a TV. I would live and work like a monk.

A month after arriving on the Cape, during which time I had subsisted entirely on home-cooked macrobiotic mush and had rarely stepped outside, I emerged with the first four chapters of a novel called *What Francis Saw*. Set in Manhattan in the year that had just ended, it told the story of an aspiring novelist who happened to bear a striking resemblance to me. Like the protagonist of most first novels, Francis Barton was strikingly passive, confronting life almost exclusively through his eyeballs. Hence, the lousy title.

I continued work on the book when I got back to New York, and two years later it was finished. In twelve chapters, each depicting a month of 1984, young Francis staggered through his dismal existence, trying to make sense of a universe in which there seems to be no place for him or his lofty ideals. The novel was six hundred pages of deeply felt, closely observed, lyrical brilliance — meaningful only to me.

It is hard to imagine it now, but in those days multiple submissions were considered a breach of authorial protocol, so I was forced to dole out my unsolicited masterpiece to one agent or editor at a time, each of whom took months to read it. Four years later, all I had to show for my persistence was a dozen rejection letters. So much for challenging destiny. I would, indeed, die a proofreader.

Smash cut to Los Angeles, ten years later. Having given up writing prose, I am now a successful screenwriter, driving the flagship of the Volvo line. I live in a beautiful house and have just had my finest original screenplay turned into a big Hollywood movie. Polished by another writer just a few days before shooting, the script that made it to the screen followed my story exactly, was ninety percent my dialogue, and was credited entirely to me, and yet it bore as much resemblance to my vision as a dangling car deodorizer does to an actual pine tree. It was a commercial disappointment and a critical calamity.

A good time to pause and take stock of my life. My thinking ran like this: if a screenplay that had been my calling card for two years, earning me millions of dollars in assignments, could be rewritten at the last minute and turned into a widely ridiculed travesty, then I would never be safe. If studio screenwriting was to bring me any sort of artistic fulfillment, it would be by chance, not by design. Pride of authorship was simply not part of the bargain.

At the time, I happened to be reading a biography of Somerset Maugham, in which I learned that Maugham's greatest novel, *Of Human Bondage*, published when he was forty-one years old, was, in fact, a revision of an unpublished manuscript of his youth. This got me thinking. What if I took another look at *What Francis Saw*? Might there be something worth reclaiming in those six hundred pages of hard work and demented solipsism? And, if there was, might a return to fiction writing, even a temporary one, be precisely what I needed as an antidote to the mounting humiliation of my life as a screenwriter?

I sat down and reread *What Francis Saw*. Sure enough,

there was plenty of good material there, but it was usable only if I could find a way to transmute it from the self-therapeutic to the universal. Inspired once again by Maugham's example, I imagined a first-person narrator situated outside of the action, but with a passionate, vested interest in every move Francis makes. It must be someone who's always watching him, like Big Brother, and so arrogant that he narrates even his *inner* life. But why would another character invest so much energy in my lost, lonely protagonist? Simple: he's madly in love with him.

Out of *What Francis Saw,* I fashioned a new novel called *Christopher.* As the lovelorn narrator revealed himself to me, I made a conscious decision not to control him, but to let him stand up, walk around, and introduce himself to me. The result was Bryce Kenneth Troop (B.K. for short), a tall, fat, bald, freckled, middle-aged, erudite, witty, unemployed, chemically imbalanced, gay alcoholic who loves the sound of his own voice. As I am not much of a typist, it was all I could do to keep up with him.

Despite constant self-doubts and the lure of high-paying screen work, I kept at the book no matter what, letting B.K. lead the way. Because I was building atop a well-laid foundation, *Christopher* did not take me another two years to write. It took less than one. When I was finished, instead of sending it off to a slush pile, I sent it to my film agent at William Morris, who immediately forwarded it to the New York office and into the hands of Ginger Barber — a legend of the profession. She took it away with her for the Fourth of July weekend. A few days later, she called and said she would like to represent it.

One Friday afternoon, as I was driving off the Warner Brothers lot after a script meeting, I received a call from Ginger telling me that Broadway Books, a division of Doubleday, had made an offer on *Christopher*. At this point in my career, I had enjoyed plenty of good news, some of it involving obscene amounts of money, but no professional call had ever made me even half as happy as this one. (And none since.) As I drove home, I marveled that all those long, hopeless hours in my twenties, hunched over a manual typewriter, had actually amounted to something. A lesson I like to pass on to young writers: hard work is rarely wasted. Hold on to every scrap you write. You never know what you'll make of it down the road.

The publication of my first novel did not turn out to be the fairy tale I had long imagined it would be. A few weeks after I had signed the contract, Ginger revealed to me that my gay editor was so excited to have discovered what he assumed to be a new gay author that she advised me not to breathe a word to him of my heterosexuality. I am candid to a fault, so the thought of living in the straight closet was anathema to me, but I reminded myself that an author's sexual orientation really ought to have nothing to do with the acceptance of his work. If readers were so narrow-minded as to hold my straightness against me, then they weren't entitled to the truth, were they? After all, it's not like I had chosen to be straight. Given the lack of wit, aesthetics, and easy sex, *who would?*

When *Christopher* came out, I appeared on gay radio shows and gave readings at gay bookstores. *The Advocate* picked it as one of the best reads of the summer. *The Chicago Free Press* called it "one page after another of witty, outrageous, raunchy, insightful, tender, and romantic prose." *Instinct* warned: "You'll find yourself cracking up and thanking your higher powers that you aren't this much of a flaming queen!" And yet, aside from a rave in the Sunday *Los Angeles Times*, the mainstream press hardly noticed the book at all. The chain stores stuck it in back, in the Gay section.

Then my friends started to weigh in. When talking about the book, women rarely even mentioned B.K.'s sexuality. Gay male friends were openly delighted by the literary ventriloquism. It was only my straight male friends, all of them ostensible liberals, who expressed dismay. Some refused to read the book. Others thought I was nuts. I mean, what if people confused me with B.K.? What if people thought I was gay? Others, more open-minded, merely expressed the polite hope that my second novel would be more mainstream.

It wasn't.

It was also narrated by B.K.

So was the one after that.

Allison Burnett is a novelist, film director, and screenwriter, living in Los Angeles. He recently directed the screen adaptation of his novel *Undiscovered Gyrl*.

For more information, go to www.allisonburnett.com.

THE HIGH PRICE OF NOVEL WRITING

Ron Cooper

My route to writing novels was circuitous and unorthodox compared to writers who have the good sense to start young. Although I took creative writing as an undergraduate at the College of Charleston and fancied myself a poet, I decided to study philosophy in grad school and was branded with a Ph.D. from Rutgers in 1990. That experience proved seminal to writing my first novel when I had a hallway chat with then-beginner novelist Rebecca Newberger Goldstein. She gave me great advice, but she didn't (perhaps couldn't) warn me of the price of novel writing.

A backwoods Southern kid in the faraway land of New Jersey, I feared I'd plunged in way over my head. Having doubts for nearly a year about my career path and abilities and wondering if I'd have done better to pursue an MFA, I began to think that my experience could be good grist for a novel mill: philosopher with redneck roots and tastes for snuff and professional wrestling gasping at the rarified academic air. This idea was more a balm for misgivings than a plan for a book, but it gelled into something more substantial when I bumped into Goldstein, who was then an adjunct in the

Rutgers philosophy department.

Goldstein's first novel, *The Mind-Body Problem*, had recently appeared. I told her about my idea for a philosophical novel. I even already had a title in mind, *Hume's Fork*, which, like her book's title, is a philosophical term. She kindly listened with what appeared to be genuine interest and gave me some well-needed advice. First, take your time. Do your research, and edit, edit, edit. Second, write a novel that has some philosophy, not a philosophy book with some characters. If readers are interested primarily in philosophy, they'll read Aristotle. Finally, don't write like a philosopher, at least, not like most philosophers. Good literary style and common academic style rarely meet. Lucky for her, I had no way of knowing then that she would write five more novels, a collection of short stories, and two biographies of philosophers (and surely more books in the future) and become a MacArthur Fellow, or else I would have pestered her to no end.

Her first bit of advice was easy for me. I'd already planned to spend two or three years working on the book; after all, I wanted to finish grad school, so I had a great deal of course work standing in the way of getting a novel written. It turned out that I did little writing on the book but a great deal of scribbling. I got into the habit of carrying around pocket-sized notebooks into which I jotted down ideas for scenes, bits of dialogue, character sketches, etc. I'd filled about a dozen of these little notebooks by the time I sat down and forced myself to write the manuscript seventeen years later. What sparked me to plant myself before the keyboard was (1) joy from reading Salman Rushdie's *The Moor's Last Sigh* in the spring of 2002 and thinking, "Damn, it's got to be fun to write something like that" and (2) fear that I'd become that guy who rattles on all the time about the novel he's writing. Since I'd thought about my novel over all those years and had all the major scenes mapped out in my head, I wrote the first draft in four months.

Goldstein's charge to make sure the story came before the ideas was tougher to pull off. Wouldn't everyone benefit from introductions to the great thinkers, even if watered down in fiction? Much of what I edited from the draft was philosophical argument and explanation, and I gauged each cut a sacrifice on the order of Abraham's binding of Isaac. Goldstein was absolutely correct, though, and I probably should have eviscerated more. A number of readers told me that the philosophical passages were difficult or, worse, boring. Lesson learned. For my second novel, I was sure to keep the philosophy subtler and better integrated.

While ruminating so long over the novel made the first draft easy to excrete, it conflicted with my main diet of academic reading and writing. Those were the salad days of my teaching career, a period in which I played the academic publishing game fairly well, producing a book (*Heidegger and Whitehead: A Phenomenological Examination into the Intelligibility of Experience*, highly praised by both its readers) and a handful of essays in scholarly journals, and during which I chewed through a multitude of dreadful articles and books to keep pace with the shifting trends of the academy. After working on such stuff, I'd need a cooling down period of a few days to purge myself of the tendency toward turgidity and obfuscation so favored in that game. Often I'd write a few sentences and realize that I'd replaced my imagined literary audience with an imagined panel of academic judges. I'd notice that instead of writing, "We rode the bus together in silence for the first four weeks," I'd write, "Our verbal discourse lay under erasure for an endurance of a lunar cycle of public transport." I bemoaned inadequate time to study my favorite writers (Twain, Faulkner, O'Connor, Hannah, Crews) and learn enough from them to develop my own prose style. I somehow managed to steal an hour or two each day, largely due to my English professor wife who, in addition to providing keen criticisms (on my writing, too!), gave unflagging support and encouragement.

Neither Goldstein nor anyone else prepared me, however, for the psychological results of spending many hours alone at what is — let's admit it — a selfish and self-absorbing endeavor that can lead to tremendous emotional damage. Only after years of writing have I realized that my anxious spells of agonizing over the quality of my work had less to do with whether it merited the literati's attention and more to do with whether those hours away from my family were worth it. I suspect that other first-time novelists merrily toil in their corners, oblivious to the inevitable approach of guilt that will bitch slap them if not during the first then surely about halfway through the second novel. We don't reveal this in public very often, but when I'm with my novelist friends after a few beers, the topic of writer's remorse is sure to surface. The discussion transforms into a therapy session as we assure each other that we are not alone with our self-reproach, that we are all in the same anxious boat, that these feelings come with this noble territory, and (after enough beers) that our suffering is the price we pay for art.

We know, of course, that our comforting words are bullshit. We know that our ways of coping more worked themselves out than resulted from any reasoned response — maybe writing only when the kids are asleep or no writing on the weekends — that seem like fair time management plans really are not. We fall prey to self-deception and tout the old "quality time" canard so popular with yuppie couples in the '80s and '90s to assuage their guilt for leaving their children in the hands of strangers staffing nurseries and day cares. We think, "Each hour writing is an hour I'm not playing 'Uno' with the kids or not having a nice dinner with my spouse, but I'll just make the hours I do spend with them extra special." Right.

Fortunately for me, my children were small, ranging in age from three to nine, when I wrote my first novel. I could write at night after they went to sleep, or in the morning before they woke up. I *could* do that, and often did, but I also sometimes wrote on weekends and sometimes in the afternoon. Fortunately for me as well, the first draft took only several months; so, by the time the remorseful feelings crept upon me, I was done with the intense writing. The guilt, however, had burrowed deep.

I wrote my second novel a couple of years later, and guilt coiled in me like a worm, as Sartre says about nothingness in the heart of being. The dual-directional tug of family versus artistic calling yanked me in twain. I could no longer deceive myself into believing that my wife and kids didn't miss me. Besides, did I really want to believe that? During that period I succumbed to the malady common to many of our ilk — depression. I can't say for certain that my condition was the result of the rigors of the novel, the self-imposed seclusion, the doubt of one's abilities, and above all, the guilt, but I'm sure they contributed. My internal anguish grew for months before I finally sought help, just in time, I believe, to prevent my becoming another casualty to the writing life.

When I give workshops for people who are thinking of writing a novel, among other things I say this: (1) Do not listen to anyone who says that writing is easy, that you should listen to the Muse, or that you should let the work flow out of you. I got news for you. Writing is hard as hell, the Muse died with Virgil, and if something is flowing out of you, seek medical attention. If you do not face constant frustration while trying to form a sentence and do not feel dread each time you approach the keyboard, you are probably doing something wrong. (2) Marry the right person. Find someone with boundless patience, someone who will abide your ill temper and still give you encouragement. It'll be tough to find someone like that who is also a terrific editor and critic. I already have her. (3) Your work will take a great toll on your psyche. Get a therapist now. You may try to self-medicate with liquor, but enough Scotch to fix you up would be more expensive than therapy.

Writing has become, for me, both friend and antagonist. While writing my third novel, still struggling with the old issues, I followed my psychiatrist's advice to recognize and relish those moments when writing makes me feel at my best. Despite depression, at times I've felt genuinely happy when writing. Despite my belief that I was engaging in an activity that contributed to my despair, writing could be an outlet through which I could exorcize my demons. Now that I'm working on a fourth novel, I've made further peace with writing by revamping Goldstein's advice to take my time: Take your time — the world is not waiting for your novel. I am a college professor, which means that I do not depend upon my writing to pay the bills. I resist the urge to write every day, and when I write I do so for only an hour or so at a time. The world is doing just fine so far without this next book.

Ron Cooper grew up in the swamps of the South Carolina Low Country but now makes his home in Ocala, Florida, where he teaches at the College of Central Florida. Trained in philosophy, which led to years of producing dreadful academic treatises, he now writes fiction laced with a philosophical flavor. His novels *Purple Jesus* and *Hume's Fork* are available from Bancroft Press. His newest project is a "gospel" from the point of view of Jesus' twin brother that he hopes will cause a scandal.

For more information, go to www.roncooper.org.

WE'RE ALL SCREWED

Anna David

The reason I decided to write a novel is that a girl I'd known and long felt competitive with did it first.

This girl always seemed to be one step ahead of me. We started working at magazines around the same time, but while my career was waylaid by self-destruction, addiction and the requisite firings that go along with that, hers seemed to cruise along.

I knew this girl because we shared a best friend. But while my friendship with our mutual friend deteriorated (turns out self-destruction and addiction aren't ideal for healthy friendships, either), theirs remained intact — as far as I could tell from the gossip which filtered back to me, combined with what I could determine via book acknowledgments and social media stalking.

But I'd cleaned my life up, found sobriety and figured out how to have friendships without sucking the very life out of a person. I was working as a writer. I was happy with what I'd accomplished.

And then this girl went and published a novel. Christ.

She was always thinking of new things and doing them. Once I heard about her book, I started to obsess over the fact that she'd written it and found myself searching for ever more information that she was, in fact, better than me. I even found some.

Then I was struck by a thought that has arguably motivated me more than any other:

If she could do it, so could I.

I'd read a lot of books, hadn't I? I'd majored in Literary Writing in college, for God's sake. Yes, I'd chosen the subject because it had sounded so fantastically easy (*No tests? I just write stories?*); but that didn't change the fact that I'd done it. My mom, who'd been an adjunct professor in my youth, had a Ph.D. in English Literature and a published dissertation. I had even wanted to be a novelist when I was little, before I got practical and realistic, and had resented the six-year-old girl featured in our edition of the *Guinness Book of World Records* because she was listed as the World's Youngest Novelist. "Her family was probably very well connected in publishing," I remember my mom consoling me. I think I was eight.

The idea of writing a novel continued to grow on me. I couldn't turn up any actual qualifications for novelists — no tests you had to pass or degrees you needed to have. And I felt I had a good story to tell: my own. I was someone who'd been wild much of her life, someone who always loved to have a good time, someone who no one ever thought would amount to much and then eventually, and shockingly, someone who holed herself up in her apartment ingesting cocaine the same way that Japanese man who's always winning those hot dog eating contests ingests Oscar Mayer. Rather suddenly, my life got very small and sad. And then, amazingly, I got sober. And happy. Recovery was nothing like I'd expected it to be and, even more surprising, *I* was nothing like I thought I would be. I'd long perceived of myself as sort of effortlessly cool and bitchy. Turned out I was kind of nice, incredibly determined and completely anal, sharpened number two pencil at the ready: a competitor who hadn't known she'd been worthy of entering any competitions. Addiction had been masking my inner Tracy Flick.

Getting sober also introduced me to a new career concept: I was suddenly employable. And, as irony would have it, my first sober job was as a staff writer for *Premiere* magazine where I would write a column called "Party Girl" that documented the premiere and awards show circuit. In other words, I was hired to spend my days perpetuating a role I had been playing, up until I got sober the previous month, my entire life. While I only had that job for a year and had already moved on to freelance writing when I decided to write a novel, the basic idea of what had happened to me — a party girl gets hired to write a column called "Party Girl" right when she realizes she's an addict and gets sober — seemed like a solid premise.

I didn't have an outline. I knew nothing. I just sat down and wrote.

A Million Little Pieces came out while I was writing my book but it didn't make me doubt my quest — or question whether doing a novel over a memoir was wise. In other words, I stayed pure to what I thought was better, rather than alter what I was doing because it might be a more strategic business move — something I don't think I've been able to do since.

I wrote about things that had happened to me and things that could have happened to me. I made up characters based on the people I knew and then came up with some fictional ways to connect each of these scenes together. I'd heard a writer once say that he tried to write three pages a day so I gave myself that as a goal. As far as I recall, I enjoyed myself tremendously. Now, I'm an exceedingly practical person as well as a person who's been yanked around Hollywood writing for free on projects that in retrospect were never going to come to fruition, so I honestly don't know exactly what I told myself as I cranked out those three pages every day. I think I just liked doing it.

At one point in the year I spent writing that book, a friend — the only friend I had at that point who had published a novel — casually mentioned that novels followed a three-act structure. I nodded cavalierly, not letting on that she was telling me something I in no way knew. Scripts had a three-act structure, I knew that, but novels? Huh. I went home and looked at the 200-odd pages I had written, realizing that I had basically written one act. So I axed about half the pages and kept writing.

Every now and then, I'd pick up a book on writing — even just a spiritual, Annie Lamott type of book about how I should embrace my words like they were the air I was inhaling. And every last one of them left me with the same feeling: panic. Or fear. I would be immediately intimidated by all the advice on how to do something I was already doing. *This is way harder than I thought*, I'd think. *I clearly don't actually know what I'm doing.* So I'd put that book down but not my own.

I'm not sure if that friend who'd published a novel has any idea how crucial her encouragement was back then. Because I'd have my moments — moments where I'd ask myself who the hell I thought I was, what made me fancy myself a novelist, where exactly I got off believing I was capable of doing something that most everyone seems to believe they can do but few in fact can. I would express these doubts to this friend and she always casually swept them aside. "Oh, your book'll sell," she would say. "I promise." I'm someone who will believe anyone telling me anything, so long as they say it in an authoritative tone. This has caused me more problems than you can imagine. But when it came to writing my first book, one "Your book'll sell" would get me through at least a few chapters. And I didn't think about anything beyond the book sale. Much like your average rom-com that stops when the couple gets together, my thoughts about my book ended with the deal my future agent would make. After that, I must have imagined — what, exactly? Riches? Fame? Some fairy tale starring J.K. Rowling or Elizabeth Gilbert? I'm not entirely sure.

And then, miraculously, it did sell. Only later did I realize how much of a miracle it all was. The path went like this: in the month that I was wrapping up the book, two literary agents happened to read freelance articles I'd written and emailed me to see if I wanted representation. I cannot express how random this was except to say that I have not had agents email me out of the blue before or since. I gave each of them the book. Both wanted it, so I chose the agent I liked best and, within a month, she had sold it to my top choice publisher.

And that's where my story got remarkably un-Cinderella-like. Within a year — five months before my book's release date — that top choice publisher was fired and her whole imprint dissolved. But I was lucky, I was told. HarperCollins was still going to publish my book — through a division the company created just to release this high-profile publisher's books. By the time of the release, there was no marketing or publicity or editing department to resent for not doing enough to support the book because there were no marketing or publicity or editing departments in existence. Writers call having their editor leave their publishing company being "orphaned." What happened in my case, I guess, is that I was orphaned and then the orphanage burned to the ground.

I continued to write and publish after that: another novel, then an anthology and then a memoir. But something had happened to me when it turned out that Cinderella's slipper hadn't fit after all: I'd become crippled by self-doubt. Every criticism lobbed at my first book seemed to stick to me. Every struggle after my publisher went out of business — and *everything* in my publishing career was a struggle after that — cloaked me in victimhood and disappointment. Every "chick lit" label clung. Every pass from every magazine I'd worked at — and from which you'd better believe I begged for a review — I dimly accepted like it was a telegram of death.

I tried to pull the arrows out but they stuck — not in my

heart but in the space that connected my heart to my fingers. I could still write but I would hear those negative voices echoing in my head and imagine the best words I could come up with being summarily dismissed as shallow or silly as I typed them. My mom's comment that she couldn't believe I had the balls to write a novel — "I mean, Jane Austen wrote novels" — would pass through my mind. None of this would shut me down entirely. It would all just float in the air, like a conversation between two people trying to keep it down while sitting behind me in a café — voices of people who, while trying to be quiet, are actually all the more irritating as they shush each other because "that lady over there is trying to work." Writing became, if not painful, then at least a bit joyless. I still did it, because on some level I felt like I had to, because it's the way I process, because I didn't know what else to do. And I told myself that I was lucky, that many people dreamed of being able to make a living writing and that I had nothing to complain about. But for a long time, I was screaming this into an empty tunnel. I obsessed over other writers' book successes and relished in my resentment toward the editor or publicist or Barnes and Nobles book buyer I felt had caused me to end up where I was.

Then, at some point, something changed. I was driving a Mini Cooper back then, a car that was still new and cool enough that we Mini drivers would automatically wave at each other on the road, silently communicating to one another that we could be friends because we shared a certain sensibility. And one day it occurred to me that if I could find a friend in someone I would never meet just because we'd both decided to get the same unsafe, impractical but unabashedly cool car, I could certainly find friends among the people who'd chosen the same unsafe, impractical but unabashedly cool (at times) career.

And I realized something else: even if my first book had been the runaway success I felt certain it should be, even if everyone had loved every word of it and I'd finally gotten the validation from my family I'd always craved and my life had changed overnight — well, then I'd have to do the same thing all over again or live with the horrific panic that my greatest accomplishment was behind me.

I'd essentially realized that as writers, we're all screwed. Or blessed. Or whatever word you want to use. We're all in it together.

When I realized that, I just got it — not only in my head but somewhere in the space that connects my heart to my hands: when I allow myself to be stifled by the perception that the world hasn't embraced my work the way it should, obsess over an Amazon reviewer giving my book one star while raving about Justin Bieber fan fiction or resent another writer for getting something I feel I deserve, I'm missing the point. Anyone getting anything in this business is a miracle. And it's like they say in the rooms of recovery: we all get our turn. If I stop attaching meaning to it all — stop getting my motivation from what other people are doing, stop believing that a successful book will bring me the everlasting joy that never comes from anything you can read in *Publishers Weekly* — I can relish in the fact that I get to type words on a page and call it a living. My books are never going to undo the damage from my childhood, bring me everlasting bliss or sell as many copies as I want them to. No one ever said they would; I just decided they would and then grew resentful when they didn't.

I don't know what's become of the girl who originally motivated me to write my first novel. Somewhere along the way, I stopped keeping track.

Anna David's books include the novels *Party Girl* (Harper, 2007) and *Bought* (Harper, 2009), the anthology *Reality Matters* (Harper, 2010), the memoir *Falling for Me* (Harper, 2011) and two Kindle Singles: *Animal Attraction* (Amazon, 2012) and *They Like Me, They Really Like Me* (Amazon, 2013). Her biography on the actor Tom Sizemore was released in April 2013 from Simon & Schuster.

She's written for *The New York Times, Los Angeles Times, Details, Women's Health, The New York Post, Premiere, People, Us Weekly, Maxim, Vanity Fair, Cosmo, Redbook, Self, Stuff, TV Guide, Teen Vogue, Variety, The Daily Beast, The Huffington Post, Buzzfeed,* and *Salon,* among many other publications and has appeared repeatedly on the *Today Show, Hannity, Attack of the Show, The Talk, Dr. Drew, Red Eye* and various other programs on Fox News, NBC, CBS, MTV, VH1 and E. Counterpoint/Soft Skull will release an anthology of the essays read at her hit monthly storytelling show, *True Tales of Lust and Love,* in February 2014.

For more information, go to www.annadavid.com.

THE EVOLVING FORM

John Dufresne

I began writing my first novel, *Louisiana Power & Light*, before I knew I had, by writing a short story called "The Fontana Gene," which I wrote when the editor of my debut collection told me we needed one more story to finish off the book. I set this story where I had begun writing it — in Monroe, Louisiana, where I had lived for several years while teaching five sections of composition each semester, off the tenure track, at Northeast Louisiana University. When I wasn't evaluating compositions or walking the baby or writing my stories, I was doing research on Monroe with the idea of eventually setting a collection of interwoven stories there. Research in those days meant getting up from the chair, leaving the house, and driving down to the parish library in the oil-burning Datsun to scour through the history of Monroe and Ouachita Parish in the microfiche files. I made notes about historic events, wrote about the flora and fauna, the folkways and "foodways," the personalities, the landscape, and the architecture. Then I found myself a benighted and chronicle-worthy family and named them after a road on the south side of town, the Fontanas. And I set out to sketch a history of the clan beginning in 1832 to the present.

I chanced on a central character when I was drinking a beer and watching the five o'clock news one day and saw a feature on a local man who had kidnapped his child from an elementary school. There was the trouble I needed. I was off.

I sat at the kitchen table, wrote about the fictive kidnapping, and wondered about what kind of trouble had led to this desperate behavior. I wrote about the dad, the boy and the boy's mother. I worked at the story a while, and I seemed to be going nowhere plot-wise (no surprise there) when I had my narrator say something about Billy Wayne, my central character, that I didn't already know. (And this may have been the moment, there at the kitchen table, that I became an honest-to-god writer or felt like I had anyway.) What came to me nearly whole cloth, with some minor tinkering, was what would be the opening sentence of the story and subsequently of the novel's first chapter:

"When Billy Wayne Fontana's second wife, Tami Lynne, left him for the first time, he walked into Booker T. Washington Elementary School, interrupted the fourth grade in the middle of a hygiene lesson, it being a Thursday morning and all, apologized to Miss Azzie Lee Oglesbee, the substitute teacher, fetched his older boy, Duane, and vanished for a year and a half from Monroe."

I say it came whole cloth, but that was, of course, after I'd been taking notes and scribbling for a long time. I pushed the chair back from the table and looked at what I'd wrought: two wives and two children, submerged trouble and palpable trouble, an adventure for a year and a half, and a return, a second split. I began to ask questions. Why not take the two boys? Who was that first wife? Why would this Tami Lynne take Billy Wayne back after what he'd done? Why would she leave him again? And who was that voice telling the story? (And that Azzie Lee, she'll need to come back to the story somehow, won't she?) I started answering the questions and wrote blissfully for some weeks, but then we packed up and moved to Binghamton, New York, and then the next year moved again to Augusta, Georgia, where Cindy and I taught at Augusta College and Tristan spent his days eating grits and greens, refusing to nap, and acquiring a Southern accent at the day care center on Walton Way. The story languished while we moved, and while I searched for and found an agent, and then ran a writers' conference, and applied for jobs and lots of other excuses not to write.

While we were in Augusta, W.W. Norton agreed to publish the book of stories, *The Way That Water Enters Stone*, and I set to work revising them. We moved again, to Florida — lured by a fabulous job in a creative writing program that I was probably not qualified for. That's when my editor Jill requested the additional story, and I took out the mountain of Fontana notes and carved out a story over several months about the last member of the Fontana clan.

I wrote then, and I still do, with a fountain pen. (Eventually, I type the manuscript with four fingers.) I owned a secondhand Atari computer by that time, but was afraid to use it. I felt more comfortable with the Brother portable word processor that allowed me to see a line at a time on a small LED screen and to correct my innumerable errors immediately. I still have it. The book went into production, and I was over the moon.

Jill called and asked if I had a novel to send her. I said I didn't, but I did have some more stories. There was a pause on the line. She repeated her question. I said, a novel? Sure. I'm working on one; which was not a total lie, actually. "Let me tinker with it and get back to you," I said. I had 150 pages of a typed novel-in-progress that I'd fooled with back in Louisiana. All I can remember about it is a boat ride taken by the inmates of an asylum off the coast of New England. *Gilligan's Island* meets *One Flew Over the Cuckoo's Nest*? I pulled it out of the desk drawer and dusted it off. I made a copy and sent it to my agent, Dick McDonough, and asked him what he thought. A week later came his response: "The drawer was a good place for it." Okay then, Plan B.

The truth was I didn't know how to write a novel. I had been trained, as it were, to write stories. I loved stories. The only way to learn how to write a novel was to write one. Time to put the Fontana notes to work again. So I had my central character, Billy Wayne, and my narrator — a first-person plural voice of the town that I'd stolen from Faulkner's story, "A Rose for Emily." I had notes on generations of Fontanas. I thought I'd get to know them better. I'd need to give Billy Wayne more trouble. Easy enough. And I decided he needed a friend, a sounding board, a foil, so I found him one, and that's when things began to go wrong.

I based my new character on a person I had seen in Athens, Ohio. I was visiting a friend and fellow writer who was then teaching at Ohio University. On this day, a highly anticipated Grateful Dead album was released, and the tie-dyed Dead Heads swarmed the record store on State Street. My friend was a vegetarian, and we were heading for Casa Nuevo for enchiladas negras. I saw a very little man selling newspapers on the sidewalk. I said, "Who's that?"

My friend said, "That's Uncle Me."

"He's who?"

"His grandfather is also his father."

My eyes may have widened and glazed over.

My friend smiled. "Everyone in town is trying to write that story."

I said, "First one published gets it."

And that's how Uncle Me became Billy Wayne's best friend. For a while. Uncle needed something to do, so I had him publishing (rather than selling) a local weekly newspaper and writing all the stories. But he wasn't breathing on the page, so I gave him more to do. He played King Lear in a community theater production. He ran for public office. He was still flat, and I realized that it was not his fault, but mine. I couldn't get past the exploitation of his size and lineage in order to honestly explore his life. And I had to get rid of him. Now I had 170 pages to rewrite. He flunked the audition, you could say.

Hotson Taylor passed the audition. I needed a cab driver to get Billy Wayne and his bride back to their motel for the wedding celebration. Hotson looked like Roy Orbison. He was trying to quit smoking. He subscribed to a progressive newspaper called *In These Times*, as I did. I found him so intriguing that I let him stick around for the next scene and

the next. He was there until the end of the book in the role I
had designed for Uncle.

By that point I had two hundred or so pages, and I wasn't
quite sure what the plot was, but I had lots of trouble. I'd
written about dozens of the cursed lives of my benighted clan.
I knew that the townsfolk were in collusion with the Catholic
church to make sure that Billy Wayne was the final Fontana. I
knew a lot about the antics of Peregrine Fontana following the
War Between the States, but I didn't know what Billy Wayne
did for work. By then he had surrendered to the charms of
Earlene deBastrop and turned his back on the priesthood.
He was a daddy of two boys, but how did he earn his living?
Well, what kind of work did I know about? I wrote stories,
but I didn't want him to. I taught, but he had no training. I
had painted houses for years, so maybe . . . My father worked
all of his adult life for the power company in Massachusetts
— the Electric Light, we called it. So I figured Billy Wayne
could do that, and if I ever had a question about the job, I'd
call Lefty. Then I realized that our power company was called
Louisiana Power & Light! What a gift. Power and light! I
spent the next two weeks researching all of the denotations
and connotations of those two magnificent nouns, filled a
manila file folder with material and set out to use the words
in every conceivable way that I could in the book. So now
Billy Wayne had a job, I had a title and the story had two
powerful themes. (By the way, the company is now called
Entergy — I lucked out in my timing.)

I wanted Billy Wayne's quest for power and light to
be at the center of the book. In that way I could explore

the compelling spiritual themes of sin, curse, confession, atonement, forgiveness, and the dark night of the trembling soul. My unhallowed novel, to my surprise, was becoming markedly religious. I went with it, lapsed Catholic that I was. So each morning I sat at the kitchen table, and wrote while playing Gregorian chants, the sacred music of my childhood. And I began the writing day by reading passages from the Old Testament, Song of Songs and the Psalms, especially. And then I might read a little Emily Dickinson or Walt Whitman. I was trying to write like Chekhov said we should: calmly, as if we were eating blinis. But I was becoming anxious. Here I was two years into the writing, and I had no idea where I was headed, if anywhere. My guiding principle had been *writing is an act of discovery.* The story will emerge as I compose. But discovery, alas, is not enough for the reader. We need revelation. And revelation assumes a destination. Where was I going? I desperately needed the sense of an ending. Structure is always the key.

I had already sensed the coming tragedy and knew that some folks were not getting out alive, but I also understood that that wasn't enough. I needed, or I wanted, the insinuation of hope at the finish, and I found that hope I needed in the title of the short story — that perdurable Fontana gene. Billy Wayne would not, in fact, be the last of his line.

The manuscript I sent to Jill approached six hundred pages. (What was I thinking? Probably that every blessed word was inviolable.) Jill sweetly suggested that I cut the novel in half and offered some obvious, if painful, suggestions. And so I cut the family's backstory — which was so much fun to write — and focused exclusively on Billy Wayne. A couple of hundred pages gone just like that. All good writing, but none of it essential. The excised passages had already done their job and led me to my plot and an understanding of my characters and themes. I needed to write them, but no one needed to read them. I learned that what you take out of your novel is as important as what you leave in. You can't free the angel until you carve away the stone. Overwriting is essential, and so is ruthless editing.

And there was something else I learned: I'm better suited to writing novels than stories. Writing novels is easier, but it takes longer. There is less pressure. There is so much to be done that you don't have time to doubt or worry or get stuck. You're always busy and you get to follow the accidents that are anathema to short stories. And you get to live so many lives. Who could ask for more? Sometimes I think I write novels because I'm lonely and want some good friends to talk with.

So I learned how to write a novel and that I could write more. The only novel that doesn't get finished is the one you give up on, like that manuscript in my desk drawer. But now I recognize that shabby literary endeavor for what it was: a dress rehearsal for the real thing. Nothing you write is ever wasted.

John Dufresne is the author of four novels, three poetry chapbooks and two books on writing.
For more information, go to <u>www.johndufresne.com</u>.

SOMETIMES YOU HAVE TO FAIL

Samantha Dunn

A writer named Kate Braverman gave me this advice when I was first starting to write fiction: "There's the story you want to write, and then there's the story that appears on the page when you start writing. Always go with the one that starts to materialize in front of you — even if it's not anything like the story you planned to write — because it's the truer, richer tale stewing in your subconscious."

At the time it sounded like just another one of those lofty, koan-like things published writers spout off to beginning writers — things that make the process sound mystical and impenetrable, and might just be horseshit designed to scare off the competition. But it turned out to be prophecy, because I never, ever intended to write my first novel, *Failing Paris*.

When I started to write fiction, I was working as a journalist. By day, I wrote articles on how to get a better butt in five days, profiled "celebrities" like Fabio, reviewed bands no one had ever heard of — like the guys from Mother Love Bone who'd landed a new singer and now were calling themselves Pearl Jam. Whatever.

But my nights, oh, my nights. They were very much under

the influence of Latino authors like Sandra Cisneros and Rudolfo Anaya, whose voices thrilled me with rhythm and whose powerfully fixed points of view blew my mind open. Gabriel Garcia Marquez' novels of magical realism were, for me, legal hallucinogens. I ached to write like they wrote, and when I say ached I mean it was a physical yearning, a constant pain, like something was trying to gnaw itself out from between my ribcage.

After taking a series of classes at UCLA's Writers' Program, I landed in Braverman's private workshop, which at the time, in the early '90s, was "the" place to be in Los Angeles if you wanted to be a serious author. Or at least that's what Kate said. She also routinely said things like, "This is a crime against the page!" and "Have you ever thought of writing romance novels? Because surely literature is beyond you." She was to writing workshops what the Queen of Hearts was to Alice in Wonderland.

That said, most of us who stayed in that group for any length of time did go on to have careers of some note. Some of us were anointed as brilliant, deemed stars fallen from the Great Beyond. I was not one of these. I toiled over what I thought would be a series of funny, quirky, and subversive short stories set around a mythical northern New Mexico town. In this mythical town were talking dogs, dyslexic *brujas*, and a whole bunch of other kitschy characters nobody anywhere seemed to have the slightest interest in.

Then one day, one of the other writers in the workshop brought in a piece set in Paris. Her story was saturated with stilted French, clichéd Eiffel Tower images and a fawning, flat idealization of French life. Or at least that's how I remember it. Truly, I can't report on it objectively, because, for some reason, as the writer read the story about her character from Connecticut on her junior year abroad and how Mummy and Daddy's surprise visit — oopsie! — on their way to Rome had made difficulty for the character, I could feel my teeth set on edge. An emotional firestorm had engulfed me by the time the story was done.

Everyone's response to the piece was tepid, but then it was my turn to critique.

I lit into her with a barbed attack wholly unnecessary and unwarranted. I don't remember all that I spewed down upon the poor writer but I do know I finally sniffed, "This isn't how it is in Paris."

"Well, how *is* it then, *Sam?*" demanded the writer, singed, to say the least, by the blast of my critique.

I opened my mouth for the smart, sarcastic reply I surely knew would fall from my tongue, but nothing came. Not a word. In that moment, I was rendered mute. I think I realized my problem wasn't her lame first draft — God knows I'd produced enough lame first drafts myself. My problem was all that France had meant to me.

Ever since I was a child trying to read the labels on my grandmother's perfume bottles, I had been in love with all things French. I loved the literature, the cinema, the *haute couture* I knew only through the pages of the *Vogue* magazines we sometimes had money enough to buy off the rack at the supermarket. I studied French all through junior high and college, and even went to a language immersion school on a scholarship. I went out with a French guy in college largely because his parents were the chairs of the French department, and I loved practicing my French with them over dinners of *endives au jambon* and glasses of red wine that came in bottles, not screw-top jugs. In the middle of the desert in New Mexico, that felt downright sophisticated. I dreamed of a cosmopolitan life, where I was always witty and well-dressed, the kind of woman who looked like she could break into a foreign language at any moment. For most of my young life I held a vision of Paris in my mind — always in soft focus, elegant, waiting for me to assume my destiny away from the trailer park where my family lived.

As they tend to do, dreams collided with reality when I finally had the chance to live in the fabled City of Lights in my early twenties. It was beautifully breathtaking and civilized, yes, but I also encountered racism and sexism so blatant it knocked the wind out of me. I met stupidity and cruelty on the streets of Paris just like in the rest of the world. That is to say, life there was so much more complex, nuanced and ultimately richer than I ever imagined in my cotton-candy dreams.

I also met many other ex-patriots like me who had come to France with the secret hope that, if only they could master the language, they would be transformed into more interesting and different people. French itself was the elixir that would obliterate all character defects and protect us from our personal histories. It's obvious, isn't it, how that plan worked out? Living there was, for me, the greatest lesson in the old saying, "Wherever you go, there you are."

I couldn't reconcile the messy, often tragic life I knew in France with the dream I had of it. So when I left Paris, I closed the door on it. I mean I nailed that sucker shut. I didn't speak the language, didn't seek out friends I had made there. My beloved volumes of Rimbaud and Apollinaire and Camus gathered dust on the shelf. I wouldn't even order a croissant in a coffee shop.

But, back to that writing workshop. I returned home that day still burning with the need to answer the writer's question, *Well how is it then, Sam?* To say I wanted to render a story about France that was as nuanced and profound as my experience of it is too polite. I wanted something to shove in the other writer's face, a kaleidoscope formed by my words that would disturb and challenge and upset anyone who read them. I wrote for hours, feverishly, producing page after page. As I wrote, words just bubbled up, so half the time I didn't know if what I was putting down was English or French — and for once I didn't care. Sometimes I cried. Sometimes I laughed.

At the end I didn't know what I had. A mess, most likely, that Kate Braverman and the workshop participants would eviscerate me for even daring to offer. But I had nothing else, so when it was my turn, I read with my head down, just hoping to get it over with quickly. When I finished . . . silence. I looked up, bracing myself for the onslaught, but all I saw were smiling faces, some even with tears in their eyes. A smattering of applause came from a couple of friends. Kate herself said something like, "Finally. This is the blood on the page." (Really, she talked that way.)

I guess the cliché would be that I "found my voice" as a writer in that piece. I also found the story that I needed to tell, about a world that was unique to me, about characters and situations I cared about desperately. I realized that the other stories never worked because I had been trying to approximate the worlds of other writers to avoid the thorny, uncomfortable work of creating my own on the page.

I spent years redrafting and writing more, but the first line I wrote is still the first line of the book: *This is how it is.*

Samantha Dunn wrote the novel *Failing Paris,* and two memoirs, *Not By Accident: Reconstructing a Careless Life* and *Faith in Carlos Gomez.* She co-edited the short story anthology *Women on the Edge: Writing from Los Angeles,* and her essays are widely anthologized, including the Seal Press collections *Drinking Diaries* and *Dancing at the Shame Prom.* She's written for *O the Oprah Magazine, Ms., Los Angeles Times* and numerous national publications, and now works as a staff writer at the *Orange County Register.* She teaches memoir at the UCLA Writers' Program and fiction writing for the Idyllwild Arts Program.

For more information, go to www.samanthadunn.net.

THAT'S NOT WRITING, THAT'S TYPING

Dan Fante

The most difficult barrier for anyone beginning their first novel is, of course, their negative and corrosive thinking. There's no substitute for the torture of self-doubt. It will cripple the new writer and render him immobilized. Self-doubt is the darkest Dantean circle of Hell.

The next snarling troll waiting under the new novelist's desk is the need for inspiration. A substitute word for inspiration is *self-sabotage*. When I began to consider writing my first novel, I realized that my mind had somehow acquired the notion that I must be *inspired* before I began typing. It was my noggin's perfect placebo for inaction and failure.

My inspiration affliction first struck me when I finished reading *The Old Man and the Sea* by Hemingway. The simplicity and beauty of that novel left me profoundly affected. I had an almost desperate desire to write. I began having fantasies about leaving the banality of my secure sales job and fleeing to a cabin in the Sierras where I knew that if I could only be alone, absent from all distractions, I would most certainly become *inspired* to begin my opus. My deviant filibustering brain had created a baseless formula: *Inspiration,* it informed me, would be a byproduct of solitude and intense concentration. If I just had the right circumstances — if I could get the planets to line up the way I needed them to — I'd be on my way.

Before I began my first novel, I took a course that required a written assignment to pass, a short autobiography. A couple of the guidelines for completing the thing were interesting: "Do not look back at what you have written. Write for ten consecutive days, one hour per day. No less — no more."

After completing that paper I had an "ah-ha" moment. It was simple yet profound: Novels are written page by page, one page at a time. Up until then, I had considered the thought of writing a four hundred page book to be daunting and unnerving, but writing one page a day was a suddenly manageable concept. I have kept to that formula for the last twenty-five years. Some days I write five pages, some days three, but most days there is just one, or a good part of it. I do it six days a week. For me, successful writing is a byproduct of me separating my fearfulness and doubt from my own tactile ability to move my fingers on a keyboard. I stopped waiting for the phantom of inspiration long ago. That fickle imp visits writers all too rarely.

All an author needs is one good idea and fifty cents worth of discipline. My ideas for novels invariably evolve from reading other writers. Reading good writers gets my juices flowing.

So here is Suggestion #1: Write like the writer you most admire. Before beginning your novel, spend some time dipping into the books that *turn you on*, the ones that made you consider writing in the first place. Then, as you begin typing, emulate that writer's style. Imitate how he or she writes.

Is this hubris and plagiarism? Not at all. When I started what became my first novel, I emulated Hemingway. The guy had been a newspaper writer. His style had no frills and moved in short, punchy sentences. That approach had great appeal for me, so I wrote the way I thought Hemingway would write.

Then, in writing *like* Hemingway, a powerful secret was revealed: It is impossible to imitate another writer. You can only write like yourself! My own style emerged. And surprisingly, the first page of my first novel did not *sound* like Ernest Hemingway. It sounded like me. And of course my subject matter was completely my own.

Suggestion #2: Start now! If you have been considering writing a novel, you almost surely have a notion of your main character in your mind. Start today. Eliminate all distractions and begin writing something that your main character is doing, some action that will jump-start your story. It's absolutely okay to not have the storyline cemented in your imagination. Having it is helpful, but not necessary. That will come as you write. Just start with your main character.

Several times I've begun a story with my guy in a cumbersome situation, like waking up in darkness and not knowing where he is. By putting my main character in challenging circumstances, my imagination begins to discover ways to get him out of those circumstances. More writing follows naturally.

All writers discover their own process, but, first and foremost, the process involves doing.

My father, the Los Angeles novelist and screenwriter John Fante, eventually came upon a very unusual way of writing his novels. As a young man, he would use the same technique that I described above — the one that I use today. He would begin with a strong main character and a vague (or sometimes strong) overall concept for his novel. But then, over time, my dad's process changed. After his fourth or fifth novel, he began working the entire book out in his head — word for word — before putting it down on paper.

I do not recommend this. I call it the John Fante, You-Should-Be-Institutionalized, method.

It would take my father three or four months to accomplish his task. He would not write a word, but suddenly become uncommunicative and withdrawn. When asked what was wrong, he almost always would snarl and say he was *thinking,* and demand to be left alone. That was the beginning, and it would go on for weeks. We would see him staring out his office window by the hour or walking around our yard kicking rocks, muttering to himself. Soon enough our family would identify these symptoms and begin to distance ourselves from Mr. Hyde. His friends stopped calling. His favorite dog would detour when he saw Pop come up the front walkway to our house.

But then, much like a painful breached birth, in a flurry of mad angst and energy, John Fante would sit down and spill his novel out on paper, usually in about two weeks. Word for word — like a mental photocopy.

Late in his life, after he had gone blind, my father dictated his final novel, *Dreams From Bunker Hill*, to my mother who transcribed it, text perfect, commas and all, just this way.

Suggestion #3: It's okay to write badly. I make a lot of mistakes when I begin a novel. Invariably, when I start out, I am also a terrible typist. I'm not sure why this is, but I assume it is because I want to spit my ideas out on paper before I forget them. And I usually discover that I've forgotten how to punctuate, too.

While writing my first or second novel, I would often pause and think to myself: "Christ, that's just awful! You ought to be back parking cars or driving a cab!" I'd sit there at my desk, staring at what I had written, and try to talk myself out of taking sixty Ambien.

Anyway, there you have it. That's the approximate process for most of the successful writers I know. Eventually, we all had to discover that one vital secret: to just keep going. Failure — not living up to my own lofty literary standards — is inevitable. So what! I just do it anyway.

Now here's the payoff: on this journey, there will come times when you achieve something magical. It will be completely unexpected and impossible to replicate. There will be days when diamonds by-the-dozen tumble from your fingers and dance in a grand ballet across your page. You will feel a unity of mind and spirit, and you will become aware that you are a channel for something inside and outside yourself. I warn you now. Prepare yourself. On those days, you will be the happiest person alive.

Dan Fante is the author of eleven books, including five novels, a short fiction collection, two books of poetry, a memoir about his relationship with his father, John Fante, and several plays. His latest novel, *Point Doom,* is a mystery/thriller that was published in May 2013.

For more information, go to www.danfante.net.

FOUR FIRST NOVELS

JANET FITCH

When asked to write about my experience writing my first novel, I had to ask: which first novel? The one in the drawer that never was finished? The one in the drawer that was finished but never accepted for publication? The young-adult one that was written on the advice of my agent, the first one to see print —which was glorious, don't get me wrong— but not what I really wanted to do with my writing? Or my first adult novel?

My first first novel — *Lisa's Room* — was psychologically intense, with good, complex characters, and full of conflict. But at the time, I didn't have the storytelling skills that could get me across the roaring river of that story. I couldn't quite hook the rope bridge to the opposite shore. Basically, I fell into the torrent and drowned. Story sense is still my weak point as a writer, though it's grown stronger over the years. Or rather, I've learned that it's a problem I can solve, and do solve, with patience. It might look like I'm drowning, but eventually I tie that rickety rope bridge to a tree on the opposite shore, lash it down and get myself across.

Between the first and second first novels, I managed to

land an agent, based on a packet of unpublished short stories (about eighteen of them), about which he said, "This isn't really a collection, it's just a bunch of stories. But I'd love to represent you, if you ever have anything I can sell." It was he who suggested I write a young adult novel from one of those stories, a book which became the *Last of the Bourbons*.

YA was a genre just emerging at the time, following the successes of Robert Cormier, Paul Zindel and Francesca Lia Block. I liked my characters and themes in this novel — all about a girl who was a compulsive liar — and I'd learned to haul myself all the way across the river without falling in. The book made the rounds for two years before we stopped circulating it. Set in the '50s — which I see now was a poor choice for the young adult market — it was not as emotionally coherent and compelling as the first-first. It took me years to figure out what its other problems were. Suffice it to say that if I hadn't moved on to another book, I'd probably still be working on that one. I learned a valuable lesson from this experience: if something doesn't appeal to the market, especially the subject matter, move on. Don't waste too much time fussing over it, trying to "get it right." It was what it was. There are more books to write.

My third first novel was also suggested by my agent. Also YA, it was a peer-pressure book based upon a short story —definitely not YA — set in real Hollywood (the crappy one with the t-shirt shops, not the fantasy one), about my much-envied, daring best friend who'd picked up a guy in a Laundromat and later determined she had been infected with "these spider things." Oy. The book naturally varied a great deal from the short story, but the complex feelings I'd moved through with this girl, and around this incident, formed the basis of the book.

The resulting novel, *Kicks*, circulated for four years before it was purchased. It was at the upper end of young adult — back in those days, it was pretty racy, though now it would be considered mild. I basically gave up on it after year two — but my agent felt it was sellable, and because agents don't (shouldn't) get discouraged quite the way writers do, he continued to send it out. He just stopped sending me the rejections.

And, wonder of wonders, the book finally sold.

After jumping on the bed for about an hour, I had a party and put all my rejection slips on the four walls of my living room. Not just the novel rejections, ALL the rejections. "Does not meet our needs at this time." They reached from the floorboards to over my head on all four walls. And to whom did it finally sell? To an editor who was, like the protagonist's mother, a Russian émigré. Here's another lesson: you never know what's going to catch an editor's eye. Publishing isn't monolithic; each editor has his or her own background, tastes, affinities. You never know. Maybe the uncle in your book happens to go fly fishing and the editor happens to really dig trout. You just never can anticipate what will attract someone to your book.

Another incident offered a more comedic lesson. After *Kicks* came out — to pretty good reviews — I received a letter in the mail with no return address. Thinking, "hate mail," I opened it nervously. It proved to be a letter from another publishing house, praising the book, how daring it was, well-written, etc., and saying that if I ever wanted to leave my publishing house, how happy they would be to have me. Now, I looked at that letterhead long and hard. It seemed somehow familiar. So I went back into my rejection file and found what I'd been looking for. This selfsame publisher had rejected the book — saying it was too out there, too tough, too "old" for the market and so on. It still makes me laugh.

The lesson? Nobody knows anything. Don't be disheartened.

Oh, that third first novel . . . The publisher did nothing for it; it sold half of its print run of 5000 copies. Just one of those books that gets a chance to breathe life for a second before it's gone. But still, I'd finally learned to tell a story to the end, and someone had published it. How exciting was that, after all those years.

But I wanted the first novel. The real one. The adult book, something crafted, a real literary novel, like *Crime and Punishment* or *Portrait of the Artist.* Like *The Alexandria Quartet.* I wanted to write a book into which I could put everything I knew, everything I had, everything I was. And I wasn't writer enough yet to do that. I didn't just want to write something and see my name on a book cover. I wanted to make the angels weep.

I continued taking writing classes at UCLA Extension, and something called the Sherwood Oaks Experimental College, and the Squaw Valley Community of Writers. I read hundreds of writing books, both instructional — *The Art of Fiction, The Art of Dramatic Writing* — and inspirational —

The Art Spirit, and Annie Dillard's *The Writing Life,* not to mention the barrels of author interviews I sucked dry for each tiny dram of insight. *Poets & Writers* was my Bible. I attended a local writer's workshop. I tracked down a writer whose poetic language I admired, the L.A. writer Kate Braverman, and began studying with her.

I knew which direction I was going as I began readying myself for First Novel Number Four. I'd recently received a rejection from Jim Krusoe, then editor of the *Santa Monica Review,* saying, "Good enough story, but what's unique about your sentences?" It took me a while to understand what he meant, and then I got it — the sentence. The poetics of the sentence — that was the missing piece. Human nature I understood, but those sentences . . .

It was in Braverman's workshop, with its emphasis on language, that I wrote a short story, "White Oleander."

Now, in those days, I sent all my short stories to the *Ontario Review,* where Joyce Carol Oates was associate editor. I clung to the hope that one day my literary hero would run her eyeballs over my work. She was my idol. I consider her early short story collections to be my literary textbooks. So I sent them "White Oleander." A month and a half later, just as it had been with all the other stories I'd sent *O.R.,* it returned. Rejected one more time. But this time, inside that rejection envelope along with the manuscript was a 1″ x 1″ sticky Post-it note that said, simply: Good story. Too long for us. Seems like the first chapter of a novel. JCO.

JCO. Ah, those magical initials. With that little note taped to my computer, and Kate Braverman's enthusiasm for a more beautiful sentence in my mind, I plunged into the novel that became *White Oleander.* Five years later, my fourth first novel was published. My first novel, the one I wanted to write and finally had enough understanding of the art and the craft to produce.

And then? It was time to write three second novels, of course.

Janet Fitch lives in Los Angeles. After the books described, she finished the novel *Paint It Black,* and is currently completing another, set during the Russian Revolution. She no longer numbers her novels. She teaches fiction writing in the Master of Professional Writing program at USC, and at the Squaw Valley Community of Writers.

TRYING TO "CURE THE CRUELTIES OF SILENCE"*

LARRY FONDATION

I am sitting at a bar in the Bastille with my friend Matthew. It is early April — springtime in Paris. I don't remember the name of the bar, but it doesn't matter. It is our last stop for the night. Matthew is my editor at *Flaunt* magazine. The waitress is gorgeous. From Lebanon, we think. We both like sitting at the bar, but we wonder if we should have taken a table. We could talk to her more naturally, though our French isn't very good. In the morning, I will fly back to Los Angeles. It is the last leg of a tour of Lyon and Paris for my novel, *Angry Nights*, published seventeen years earlier in the U.S., and now out in France as *Sur Les Nerfs*.

In college, I didn't believe I could write. I didn't think I was smart enough, good enough. I'd gone to a decent public

---

* Gerald Vizenor — from the jacket blurb for *Angry Nights*

school, but this was Harvard; and I came from the ghetto and everyone seemed so smart.

My friend, John, came over from Dorchester one night. Dennis Lehane has described Dorchester as a place so bad, it didn't deserve to be called a place. John had a car, an old Chevy Impala — not a cool old car, just an old car, beat up and big. We tracked down a parking space on Mt. Holyoke Street. We were headed to a Harvard Square bar. As John backed up to grab the space, some rich pricks in an MG convertible darted in to steal it. John and I promptly jumped out of our car, went over to the open MG and grabbed the guys by their shirts, screaming at them, "What the fuck do you think you're doing! Move that piece of shit little car now, you fucking assholes!" They moved the car.

Squares of script on tunnel walls,
Graffiti grafted from tattooed skin,
Drunk girls stationed outside tavern doors,
Pigeons peck at torn trash bags
As the Universe continues to expand and replicate by mitosis;
My dreams look like particles but not like waves.
One girl is dressed all in red — red hat and blouse, red leather
        skirt, red high heels, red toenails:
She is the one I want.
I've been here before — that I know,
But not much else.
I sit on the curb with my blue suitcase,

Empty but for the remnants of her DNA:
Isolate flecks of time burned at the stake,
Transubstantiated at the gallows in Danvers,
Geography notwithstanding.
I pay my bill at the brothel,
Up front, on time, at the sound of the scolding bell;
My yellow sweater, the burning leaves, time begotten;
She never lets me down.

After college, while my Harvard friends went off to business
school and law school, and my Dorchester friends got truck
driving jobs or went off to jail, I signed up for VISTA, the
domestic sister to the Peace Corps. I was lonely for a while.
Then I found girls, I found my politics, and I found Hubert
Selby, Jr.

In school, I'd read Joyce with my girlfriend, Hawthorne
and Melville with my roommate, Hemingway and Fitzgerald
with seemingly everyone. I plunged into Southern writers,
and devoured Welty and O'Connor along with Faulkner
and Robert Penn Warren. Reading Kerouac aloud got me
laid. The precise imagery of William Carlos Williams made
me cry.

But I didn't know you could write about neighborhoods
like mine, about the kind of people that I grew up with —
barflies and hooligans, hookers and druggies. Yes, the Beats
wrote about drugs, but they were "becoming enlightened."
We read the requisite James Baldwin, but it was "The Fire

Next Time," not "Sonny's Blues."

I could write about John and Jeff and John, and Tina and Danny and Lorraine and Nosh (aka Noreen).

Spread out on a dingy, thrift store couch in my apartment in Somerville, Massachusetts — then known as "Slummerville," now another Harvard bedroom community — I gasped through *Last Exit to Brooklyn*. I'd read the jacket blurbs — "like the click of a switchblade knife" and "a profound vision of hell" — but I didn't believe them.

"Tralala," the fourth section of the book, begins like this:

"Tralala was 15 the first time she was laid. There was no real passion. Just diversion . . . the other girls were willing, but played games. They liked to tease. And giggle. Tralala didn't fuck around. Nobody likes a cockteaser. Either you put out or don't. That's all. And she had big tits. She was built like a woman. Not like some kid. They preferred her . . ."

I was working eighty hours a week, learning to organize in forgotten neighborhoods — Saul Alinsky style. Even at just twenty-two, I was burning myself out, though I didn't know it at the time. I still do the same work, albeit at a different pace. Popping Valium and swigging whiskey, I finished reading *Last Exit to Brooklyn* for the first time.

A few years earlier, on my first night home from college

— twelve miles and a universe apart — my friend Jeff was stabbed to death outside a bar called "Cataloni's," where we'd been drinking for years, though most of us had just turned eighteen (the legal drinking age at the time).

I heard the news over the radio as I was sitting, alone, at my parents' kitchen table.

I told my father I was going to meet my old friends for a beer. I locked the rattling door of my childhood home and jogged briskly towards the tavern.

Jeff had been sped off to the morgue by the time I got there.

Richie was kneeling on the sidewalk, covered in blood. Jeff had died in his arms. Cataloni's delivery truck boomed out of the alleyway behind the bar. They made their money delivering pizza. Their pizza is good. I remember being hungry.

Danny said, "Let's go find those motherfuckers."

"Yes," I said. I was ready to go.

Johnny Mac said no. We pushed and shoved each other.

"You're the only one of us who can get out of here. Go home!"

I hadn't realized when I signed Harvard's acceptance letter that I had also signed an exit slip from the working class, but I guess, in a way, that I had.

I skirted around Johnny Mac and jumped into Danny's car to go track down Jeff's killers.

We drove around for hours, through a damp Boston night, got drunk, got high, cried. Of course, we found no one.

Fictionalized, the incident would form the core of the first chapter of my first novel, *Angry Nights*.

After college and two years in VISTA, having never left the Northeastern United States, I decided at twenty-three to hit the road. I spent a couple of months in the car and fleabag motels until — with no money and no land left — I wound up in Los Angeles.

My travel buddy and I had a friend in Los Angeles — not in Seattle, or San Francisco, or Portland, or some other West Coast venue. Los Angeles.

We crashed on our friend's couch and we stayed. I stayed. Got an apartment, got married, had kids, bought a house. Really stayed.

And I got a job in South Central Los Angeles with Saul Alinsky's organizing network, the Industrial Areas Foundation. I organized in housing projects, among storefront churches, alongside nuns and ex-cons, in Compton. The people I worked with looked like my friends from back in Dorchester — different backgrounds perhaps, different home languages and countries of origin, but the same people — poor, struggling, tough, more likely to go to jail or to die than to go to college. And they were like Harry, and Tralala and Vinnie — the characters in *Last Exit to Brooklyn*. By then, I'd also read *Native Son*, and Nelson Algren and Donald Goines. I started to put two and two together.

The night the 1992 riots broke out, I was running a meeting at 60th and Crenshaw, the neighborhood where *Boyz in the Hood* was filmed. The leaders of my organization planned to drive me out of South L.A. in the trunk of a car. Reginald Denny had already gotten his ass kicked. Stupidly, I refused. I drove myself home that night. I drove through fire and smoke and people throwing bottles and shooting guns. I stopped at a red light. A group of guys started to rock my car. I gunned it and sped off. They shouted obscenities at me, but I was long gone. I turned left and right, and right and left, to avoid the gathering mobs. When I pulled into my driveway, my ex-wife and my wife were talking on the phone. They never talked. The next morning, my kids caught ashes like snowflakes on the front lawn. They cupped the cold cinders in the small palms of their hands. "Look, Daddy," they said. They were young.

I began to write in earnest.

I finished my un-novel novel, *Angry Nights*, and shipped it off to the FC2 National Fiction Competition. They were asking for "innovative fiction." What the hell?

Meanwhile, eighteen months later, the human disasters of 1992 gave way to the natural disaster of the Northridge Earthquake of 1994. The quake struck around five in the morning. My wife and I swayed down the stairs like we were walking on a boat in a storm. We grabbed our three kids out of their beds and huddled in the place that our contractor had told us was the strongest part of the house. I was scared in a way that I wasn't during the riots. This time my whole family was in danger. We waited out the shaking and finally it stopped.

No work, no school the next day, so we puttered around the house, calming our nerves, tensing up at the aftershocks, checking to see if everything was alright: the gas lines, the chimney, the broken glassware, the cracks in the walls. Around noon, the phone rang.

"I'm calling to tell you that you are the winner of the 1994 FC2 National Fiction Competition."

I thought it was a friend playing a bad joke. It was Curtis White from FC2.

The continuing aftershocks made it a bit hard to enjoy the moment, but the rattling stopped and the book would be published.

Almost seventeen years later, I would enjoy the moment once more — in a bar, in the Bastille, in Paris, where the Lebanese waitress was a joy to behold.

Larry Fondation is the author of two novels and two collections of short stories, all set in inner city Los Angeles. His two most recent books are collaborations with London-based artist Kate Ruth. Fondation has won a Christopher Isherwood Fellowship in Fiction Writing. His fifth book, *Martyrs and Holy Men*, was published in the Spring of 2013. His books are all appearing in France, published by Fayard.

For more information, go to www.larryfondation.com.

LOUD AND CLEAR

Jordanna Fraiberg

I first declared myself a writer when I was twenty-two. It was the spring of my senior year in college, I had just won the National Intercollegiate Squash Championship, and I was being interviewed by the student newspaper. When the reporter asked about my post-college plan, I realized I didn't have one. Without thinking, I said my dream was to waitress at a cafe in Portugal and write a novel.

I had never been to Portugal before. I had also never written anything before. And if this was my dream, it was news to me. So, I went along my merry way and ignored it.

Over the next year, I spent almost every day feeling this nagging guilt that I wasn't writing. It was a similar tug to the one I felt when I skipped a training session. The only difference was that I was an athlete, but I definitely wasn't a writer.

The guilt persisted when I went to study English literature at Oxford. I confessed this feeling to one of my advisors there, a reputable poet. I was twenty-four at the time, and he explained that he didn't start writing until he was thirty-five, that it didn't matter when you started. There was something about his words that released me from the idea that I had failed before I had even begun.

So I ignored the guilt again and moved to Los Angeles to pursue a career in the feature film business. It was perfect, I thought. I could spend my days around brilliant writers and directors, and it would magically fulfill my own suppressed creative urges.

Cut to three weeks later, and I was sitting behind a desk, with a headset affixed to my ear, on a major motion picture studio back lot fielding phone calls from Very Important People. And I was making flashcards for my film producer boss who decided he wanted to improve his vocabulary in between watching episodes of Jerry Springer.

This was definitely not what I had in mind when I imagined my Fabulous Creative Life, so I decided it was time to try writing myself. And since everyone around me was writing screenplays, I figured that was where I should start. Convinced I couldn't do it myself, I found a partner in an equally disillusioned newcomer to Hollywood. But every time he met our self-imposed deadlines, I felt myself shrinking away, paralyzed by fear and self-doubt, unable to generate anything.

I decided to forget my silly dream and to focus on getting a new job instead. And I began to date writers. But dating writers and working with writers, and surrounding oneself with writers, does not a writer make.

Less than a year into my new job, that nagging feeling started to swell again, and it could no longer be ignored. Upon a friend's urging, I signed up for a creative writing class at UCLA extension. I strategically picked a class that was both close enough to my office to make it easier not to blow off, and, in my mind, not so demanding as to be impossible to complete. That's why I took a class on the short story. I figured a short story could be as short as a page. Achievable in eight weeks. No pressure. Just show up.

Despite the fact that I almost skipped the first class, I did show up. Week after week. I did my homework, and in time, I was able to get past the cobwebs of insecurity and perfectionism enough to write something that had a beginning, a middle, and an end. And once I got into it, I kept writing stories about the same character.

After about the third or fourth class, my teacher pulled me aside one day and told me I was writing what felt like chapters in a novel. When I vehemently denied it, she proceeded to ask me what I planned on doing with the book once the class was over. "Nothing" was my first response. It was flattering, but I knew I couldn't possibly finish a novel. A few weeks later, as the class was coming to a close, my teacher pulled me aside again and told me that I had to keep going. That I had to finish.

That time I listened. And I realized that I couldn't do it alone. That I needed the support of a trusted guide. My teacher agreed to continue the class as a workshop with a few other students. We met weekly at a neighborhood bookstore, and I kept churning out chapters about this same character. Gradually, a larger narrative arc began to take shape. The rest of the students eventually dropped off, but I kept working with my teacher until I came to the end of a draft. It took two years of stopping and starting, due to work and life and a lack of belief in my ability to finish, but once I did, I knew I wasn't done.

After a few months away from the manuscript, I zeroed in on revisions. As a former athlete, I knew how to set a training schedule and to stick with it. So that's what I did. I figured out what I wanted to change and I broke it down into smaller segments.

That's when something else started to happen, too. I began to view the manuscript differently. Instead of being an outlet for my growing frustrations with my chosen career at the time, I began to secretly think of it as my golden ticket, the thing that was going to change my life. Needless to say, that was a lot of pressure for any manuscript to take. Especially my first one.

Which was why, when I finally started submitting it to agents, each rejection felt like a bullet, each one lodging itself deeper into the heart of my hopes and dreams. I had allowed my sense of self-worth to become entirely wrapped up with the book's success.

After only five rejections, I put the book away, closed the file and accepted the crushing disappointment that I was still where I was. That nothing had changed except for my own perceived potential. I knew intellectually that the rejections weren't harsh, that some were very instructive, and that the book needed more work. But what I was secretly mourning was that I thought this was the only book I'd ever be able to write. And it wasn't good enough.

So I re-focused on the fun, creative parts of my job. I

dated some more writers. But that same familiar itch, the nagging feeling that I wasn't connecting to part of myself persisted. Since I had deemed my novel writing career DOA, I decided to write and direct a short film. The experience was exhilarating, and it reminded me again of my essential need to have a creative outlet.

And it reminded me of why I loved to write.

By then, I had had enough distance from my manuscript that I was able to assess it anew. And at around the same time, a friend offered to send it to a recently promoted agent who was interested in reading it. I was excited, but that time, I wasn't looking for the book to change my life, I was looking for someone to connect to the material enough to want to talk to me. And that's what happened.

I got a call a few days later. The agent had read my book. She loved my voice and was interested in working with me on another draft. It was everything I had wanted. But when she also said she was interested in helping me with another idea if I preferred, I recognized that something in me had shifted.

I no longer wanted to publish the manuscript I had agonized over for four years. I recognized its limitations, as well as my own to make it into something more than it was: my start.

I wanted to write something else. And I was ready.

The next book I wrote became my first published novel, *In Your Room*. My second book, *Our Song*, was just published, and I'm working on a new book. I'm saying this, not to brag, or to suggest I'm a great writer but because I can finally appreciate how hard I've worked, and I can savor where I am in this moment. Not all the moments are like these. But they are important, because they remind me why I write.

It is not for accolades or for external validation or even for publication (although those things are wonderful). The true reason that I write is that it's an essential way for me to process the world. To reflect on it. And to express it in a way that connects to my authentic self. If I were a religious person, I'd say it was even a way of experiencing the divine. Not everyday. But enough that it has become an integral part of my being.

And that's why I started writing my first novel, even if I didn't know it then.

Looking back, I now realize the declaration I made on that spring day in 1994 was my subconscious speaking loud and clear. It just took the rest of me a decade to hear it.

Jordanna Fraiberg was born in Montreal, Quebec, and currently lives in L.A., where she settled after receiving degrees from Harvard and Oxford. A former national squash champion and Hollywood film executive, she now divides her time between dreaming up stories and chasing her toddler. She is the author of *Our Song* and *In Your Room*.

For more information, go to www.jordannafraiberg.com.

THE DIVIDE

SHERI HOLMAN

There are two stacks of paper on a table. Each has page numbers, each has a title. You've poured yourself into both, but one has been validated by money and the other has not. One is your first published novel, the one the world knows you by. The other is your "first" first novel. The one that got rejected — that you've since rejected like a boy who dumped you. You want to still love it, but your cheeks burn every time you look at it. You wonder what having written it says about you.

Lots of writers have a "first" first novel in the drawer. Mine is the 199 page heartfelt mess called *Seneca Falling.* I finished it in 1991 when I was twenty-five years old and trying to teach myself how to write without the benefit of an MFA program. It took as its subjects (among other things) an over-sexed failed feminist poet, a circus rhinoceros who thought he could fly, a Pentecostal girl looking for messages in double-yoked eggs, Percy Bysshe Shelley's sister-in-law, Clare Claremont, Echidna, the mythical mother of monsters, and the pain of a one-night stand. (I'd finally had one — it was painful.) To write it, I'd quit my job as a temp in a publishing house, taken my $2,000 worth of life savings and traveled to Greece because another writer I knew told me it was cheap to live there. Like my failed poet protagonist, I was trying to extricate myself from a bad relationship and saying I was leaving the country to write a novel felt better than saying my heart was broken and I was running away.

For four months, I scribbled madly in cheap domatias and in the shade of ruined temples. I spent a week writing in a white-washed convent, rising and chanting with the nuns. I swam naked in the Libyan sea and lived another week in a cave, dressing only to walk miles along a goat path where I wrote in a café and availed myself of their toilet. Words flew across the pages of my thin, gray, college-ruled notebooks, and I followed the wild leaps of story and character with as much excitement as I did the many digressions and side trips of my journey. Writing, like living, I told myself, was the act of accumulating — pages, experiences, lovers, ideas. I wrote every day with a deep intensity of purpose and no preconceived idea of what my story would be. The world was wide and I felt entitled to everything the past and present had to offer. There would be time to make sense of it all when I went home in September.

Whenever I tell this story — at college lectures or on literary blogs — about now is when I fondly roll my eyes at my younger self, returning to New York with no job, no apartment, no money — nothing but a nice all-over tan and six notebooks of supercharged prose. I'd left my bank card with a friend in case I got into trouble, and that friend had drained my bank account of the entire $800 I had set aside to start over.

In the cocktail party anecdote of this story, I look for work during the day and attempt to wrestle all those slippery ideas into a plot at night. After a few months, I land a job as the assistant to a high-powered literary agent; she reads the book and declares it a disaster. In my youthful hubris, I ask her to send it out for a second opinion and I receive back a three page single-spaced rejection letter, in equal parts devastating and encouraging. I set *Seneca Falling* aside and go to work, seriously teaching myself how to write by reading the slush pile and editing other people's manuscripts. A year later I take another trip, just two focused, circumscribed weeks to Egypt for research, and come home to write my first published novel, *A Stolen Tongue*, the story of a semi-neurotic, passionate medieval monk on pilgrimage to the Holy Land and Mt. Sinai. That book is widely acclaimed and translated into thirteen languages. Youthful folly redeemed by ultimate success.

This is a story that comforts students and other would-be writers. There's just enough struggle, just enough self-deprecation, just enough youthful excess and obliviousness. And of course, from the beginning, you know it ends happily. So what if I gloss over the despair I felt as doubt unraveled the Arachne's tapestry of character and theme I'd been weaving in the Aegean? Why mention the panic and nausea brought on by reading and rereading revisions that even I knew weren't working? The bit that never makes it into the approved first novel narrative is the night I spent at the home of my agent's former assistant. This cultured and wealthy young woman read the manuscript and invited me to dinner. "You didn't really think this was remotely saleable, did you?" she asked, puzzled, and I realized she had mistaken me for a sane person. "Does it read like any novel you've ever read?"

Every day when we sit down to write, novelists are crafting two stories at once. First, there's the love and betrayal, suspense and deception of the conscious narrative. Running silently beside it, is the story we're telling ourselves — that what we have to say is fresh, that it matters, that it's worth whatever income or relationship we're currently neglecting and sabotaging to write it. For some period of months or years we must self-hypnotize ourselves into believing we are geniuses, and probably never more than when we're making our first attempts. How else could we sit there, alone, slowly accreting pages? But then there comes a day, as happened with my "first" first novel, when we wake to ourselves. Someone gives us the kind of soul-crushing criticism we instinctively know is true, that we can't argue against, that, had we been in our right minds, we would have seen ourselves. We are stricken with a kind of existential horror — not that our book won't sell or that we've embarrassed ourselves in front of a respected reader, but that our storytelling self has fucked over our saner self. Having drunk our own Kool-aid and become lost in our own dream, the very instincts we relied upon to get us this far, have betrayed us, leaving us naked and bereft.

When I was first asked to contribute to this anthology, I had been prepared to simply recount the same light, silly story I've been telling for the last twenty years. For godsakes, I was only twenty-five. Who hasn't written a bad draft? But now at the age of forty-six, with five novels, three kids, pediatric cancer, and a divorce under my belt, I appreciate how cherished ideas of reality can turn on a dime. I feel closer to that younger uncertain self than I have in decades. The experience of getting lost and pulled up short by that first failed novel has — for better or worse — come to define my writer's personality. Maybe you'll recognize the pattern in yourself. Transgression, overreaching, blind faith and then the backlash of awakening, some joy, but more horror at what we've created, or failed to create. On the days when I am most tempted to give up this career and go do something else — anything that doesn't make my brain hurt so bad — it comes from a desire to stop having to suspend my own disbelief, to stop setting myself up, to be less internally divided. If we push ourselves as writers — and why else write? — the swift, violent perspective lurch is nothing we leave behind with a first novel. It's nothing we outgrow. If we keep doing this, we make uneasy peace with the divide between the inspired self and the censorious self. The divide becomes who we are.

Three weeks into my Greek trip, I found myself on the northern island of Thassos, mythical home to Odysseus's Sirens. It was cold and raining and I had been battling a bad cough and high fever for several days. One afternoon, during a break in the rain, I felt compelled to get out of bed and walk. I have no memory of getting through town, but I was soon wandering through a wind-twisted pine forest along a path that would eventually take me, I hoped, to the island's old amphitheater. The woods were swarming with black, biting horseflies, and, as the only meat around, I was soon bombarded. Using a broken cypress branch as a switch, I did my best to keep them from landing, but soon even the branch did no good. My arm grew tired and the flies dove at my face and savagely bit the back of my neck. Here, the fever took over. I had wandered into the woods, a sick and curious visitor, but now I became like a wild creature, trying to escape the flies. I broke into a run, not knowing where I was going, scrabbling over rocks and sliding down embankments. Part of me had let go and was blindly fleeing, but another part was consciously recounting the Io myth — Zeus' lover hounded by his jealous wife in the form of a horsefly, until Zeus took pity and transformed her into a cow. And then in a stroke that is too unbelievable even for fiction, I found myself in a grove of silver olive trees overlooking the sea.

A piercing squawk and rustle brought me up short as a turquoise peacock lifted from the branches and wheeled overhead, so close I could have plucked one of his ragged tail feathers. I was breathing heavily from the run, my sore throat screaming. Drops of rain still clung to the olive leaves, and I licked handfuls until my thirst was slaked. I heard voices and walked a little further to find I'd reached the amphitheater after all. A group of young German students performing an impromptu scene from Romeo and Juliet turned to stare at me. Abruptly, I had re-entered reality: tourists playing with history, not getting lost in it. I was able to see my wild run through the forest as a thing of sudden, alarming, precious madness. I took a seat on a slab of craggy marble and waited for my heart to still. Then I slowly walked back to my room, and wrote it all down.

Sheri Holman has written four award-winning and bestselling novels published by Grove/Atlantic, including *The Dress Lodger*, a *New York Times* Notable Book and longlisted for the Dublin IMPAC Award; *The Mammoth Cheese*, named a *Publisher's Weekly* and *San Francisco Chronicle* Book of the Year and shortlisted for the UK's Orange Prize, and most recently, *Witches on the Road Tonight*, a NYTBR Editor's Choice, winner of the Independent Publisher's Gold Medal for Literary Fiction, the 2011 Shirley Jackson Award for Best Novel, and named a Book of the Year by *The Boston Globe*, *The Toronto Globe and Mail*, and *PopMatters*. Sheri is a founding member of The Moth. Her first published novel was *A Stolen Tongue*.

For more information, go to www.sheriholman.com.

SO YOU KNOW: INSTRUCTIONS FOR A MIDDLE-AGED-ACTRESS-WANNA-BE-WRITER

Dinah Lenney

1. First of all, so you know: they — that is, other middle-aged people — will try to talk you out of the MFA. They, who already have advanced degrees or multiple books under their belts, will roll their eyes, and possibly sniff. "This seems not entirely practical," they'll say. The more ruthless of them will announce, "That ship has sailed." But you mustn't be deterred. Have the courage of your convictions, even though it sounds absurd to you, too. Don't listen to the voices in your head: *Who needs to go to school to write a book? Who doesn't have any savings? Who has two children to support? Who's playing for time because her career isn't working out and she doesn't know what to do next?* Or, if you hear them, give that other voice (your own) equal time: *Who has anything to lose? Who's as able as the next guy to take out student loans? Who ever made a practical decision — who ever did anything in her life except follow her heart?* Then go ahead and do it: show up at that low-residency program in Vermont, where your hair will frizz in June, and your ears will freeze in January; where the dorms — dorms! — will be smelly; where, for the first time in over two decades, you'll eat three meals a day in a dining hall — and *dessert* with both lunch and dinner just because it's there — and where you'll find your people, the people you might have found over two decades ago, but you wanted to be an actress, remember?

2. Take yourself seriously. You're paying for it, after all. Do not despair about whether or not you're worthy, whether or not the hordes approve, whether or not you will finish this project or if anybody will care when you do. Rediscover the person you were: that little girl who loved to make up stories, the one who lived inside of books, but who somehow got distracted along the way; who, as an actor, found safety in numbers and comfort in collaboration, and who wouldn't admit she wanted to write because she was afraid that she didn't know how — but she took comfort, remember? In a corner of page 138 of the March 8th issue of *The New Yorker,* which she cut out and saved in another city in 1982, and which still lives on the bulletin board over her desk — *your* desk! "Good writers don't necessarily write good letters, but good letter writers are always good writers," wrote critic Whitney Balliet all those years ago. About what? About whom? Don't worry about that. That isn't why you saved it; that isn't why you repeated that sentence over and over in the dark like a wish or a prayer . . .

3. Rejoice. Rejoice when you finish the manuscript. Rejoice when you sign with an agent and she sends it out wide. Twice. And when those rejections start coming in: 1, 2, 3, 4, . . .

19, 20, 21, 22, . . . And coming in all over again: 34, 35, 36, . . . 41, 42, 43, . . . Call on your experience. Remind yourself you're an actor. You know all about rejection, you spit on rejection — bah, ptooey. Brace yourself, though: they — not just the ones with the degrees and the books this time, but your actual friends and family — the people who love you — won't know how strong you are. How stubborn, how resourceful, how brave (yes, you are). *You're a writer*, they'll say, by way of encouragement. (They don't mean to patronize . . .) "Put this one away," they'll say. "Start something else." Not that they're wrong about pressing on with a new idea, but otherwise ignore them. Ask your agent, "Can we try smaller presses? University presses?" She'll answer: "*You* can." She'll release you from your contract.

4. Rejoice, damn it, you're free. Stop crying and do as you've always done. Go after what you want in spite of the odds, as if they had nothing to do with you. Because they don't.

Did you think this would be easy? Of course not. You knew better. Every time you booked a job — an acting gig — you were stunned, remember? Remember that cartoon you saved? The one from your beloved *New Yorker*, though you cannot now remember the date, or where you've filed it away. But you recall the gist: two actors sitting at a bar, and the caption read something like, *It's between me and the guy who's gonna get the part*. You didn't play Lady Macbeth on Broadway, nuh uh; you played her in a black box on La Cienega Boulevard for fifteen dollars a performance. The upshot: You don't care how you do it — it doesn't have to be

Random House or Doubleday or even Soft Skull, that hip little press in Brooklyn: you are going to find a home for your book. It's 2004. Book yourself a ticket to AWP in Vancouver. Walk up to Ladette Randolph at the University of Nebraska Press table. Catch her eye. Tell her your story.

5. Rejoice. Rejoice, when she says she will read thirty pages. Back in Los Angeles, don't even bother to figure out which thirty will work. Send the whole manuscript. Write her a funny little note by way of admitting that you can't choose — she'll have to do it for you. And you know what? After all this time, you'll only wait a week before hearing from her, in an email, that she likes your book; that she wants to send it to outside reviewers; that it's your turn to choose: she will assign the book to whomever you say. She's stacking the odds — she's telling you she wants to publish your book! And so she will. And so she does.

6. So you know? You thought this was hard? Next time will be harder. Next time you'll know too much. You'll anticipate *rejection*, yup, which is not a bit the same thing as dealing with one after another. You'll have students as well as mentors (and friends, and family) to answer to this time — you'll have long since given up acting, nothing to fall back on, ha. You'll be at the other end of middle age; not keen to take up the culinary arts, or landscape design, and surprisingly — never mind the advanced degree and the book under your belt — your faith and your confidence in yourself will be somehow diminished. You're that much closer to death, after all. You have that much less time. But you did it once and you'll do it again. And when you do? You'll rejoice.

Dinah Lenney, who has played in the movies, on stage, and in hundreds of television episodes, is the author of *Bigger than Life: A Murder, a Memoir,* and co-authored *Acting for Young Actors.* Her work has appeared in *The New York Times, Los Angeles Times, Ploughshares, Brevity, Creative Nonfiction, Agni* and many others. She serves as core faculty in MFA writing programs at Bennington College and Pacific Lutheran University, and in the Master of Professional Writing at USC. Her second memoir, *The Object Parade,* will be published by Counterpoint Press in 2014.

For more information, go to www.dinahlenney.com.

MY FIRST STOVEL

Paul Mandelbaum

My first novel was not a novel. Then, for a while, it was. And finally, thank god, it wasn't.

Here's what happened. During my final year at the Iowa Writers' Workshop, I began the book that ultimately would be called *Garrett in Wedlock* as a series of short stories. They were not at all good. So, I hid them in a drawer and distracted myself with the task of producing a literary anthology — not so unlike the one now in your hands — soliciting authors for their juvenilia.

I'd gotten this questionable idea on the eve of graduation, terrified by the prospect of facing the real world armed only with that poorly executed portfolio of stories, an undefined amount of talent, and something called an MFA degree. I did know an editor at Algonquin Books who, in my previous life as a journalist, I'd once interviewed, and she turned out to like the anthology idea when I ran it past her. She encouraged me to create a formal proposal. The proposal alone took nearly an entire year, and might never have come together if not for the coincidental death — this feels ghoulish to note — of Linda Grace Hoyer Updike, mother of John Updike.

In her attic, she had long kept a trunk full of his childhood writings, which he was just beginning to rummage through when my solicitation letter arrived. With some trepidation, he sent me the mystery novel he'd composed when he was fourteen. Precocious, charming, and inadvertently hilarious, it delivered everything an aspiring editor of literary juvenilia could hope for and was worth, finally, a book contract from Algonquin. So armed, I set about soliciting another three hundred or so authors, a process that proved to be a wonderfully effective way to avoid my own writing.

Those grad school stories hidden in the drawer . . . I hadn't been avoiding them entirely, though it might have been better if I had. Because somewhere during this period, mindful of the truism that novels sell more readily than collections, I'd embarked on a misguided attempt to shape the material I'd begun in class into a "novel." Bad decision. Somehow I'd managed to make everything worse, the results reading like a handful of half-formed short stories with even mealier filler in between. A mess, truly. Back in the drawer it all went.

By now, though, I'd received in the mail forty-two samples of famous writers' earliest efforts, including Margaret Atwood's high-school essay promoting a woman's right to smoke cigars, the werewolf parody Gore Vidal wrote at Exeter, Maxine Hong Kingston's editorial, written when she was fourteen, decrying rude manners at school dances, and a fairy tale with the charmingly misspelled title "Jhonathan and the Witches," penned by nine-year-old Stephen King. My publisher was thrilled with these contributions, and said, "Wouldn't it be great if you could provide *side notes* that would make informed connections between the juvenilia and later work?" Sure, this required extra labor, at least a year's worth, but I embraced the distraction.

And yet, I did manage somehow to reopen the drawer of banishment, this time with the more modest aim of trying to isolate whatever had so long ago convinced me each fledgling piece might be a short story. Discarding everything but those kernels, I set out to try writing just one, something with a beginning, middle, and end. And when I felt I'd done my best, I tried another. I would send these stories to literary magazines, then send the rejected manuscript, usually revised further, somewhere else. (One piece went through this process more than forty times before finding a good home.)

Eventually, I had a dozen, some told from the title character's point of view (the husband Garrett), some from his wife's, some from her children, and one, for the hell of it, from Garrett's secretary, Adriane. Individual stories, all with beginnings, middles, and ends, but still cognizant of each other and coalescing, so I hoped, into a whole greater than the sum of its parts.

I enjoy this elliptical form when other writers use it, sometimes called "linked stories," sometimes a "novel-in-stories," or, as the cover described Jennifer Egan's *A Visit From the Goon Squad* . . . well, the cover didn't call it anything at all. Not a novel, not even fiction — the editors seemed to have simply thrown up their hands (which makes the fact that it went on to win the 2011 Pulitzer Prize all the sweeter).

In my own case, however, my concern that a book of stories, linked or otherwise, would be harder to sell than a traditional novel seemed to bear out. An agent, whom I'd met through friends in the intervening years, sent it hither and yon, collecting a huge pile of rejections — again, in the range of forty places and including Algonquin, alas, though they had published the juvenilia anthology with reasonable success. As this parade of rejection passed in the background, I worked on a kind of sequel. A spinoff really, featuring that secretary, Adriane. This work also took the form of linked stories. It had taken me so long to figure out how to construct a book that way, I wasn't about to abandon it so readily.

Meanwhile, I'd come across a review of someone else's novel that made the book sound like it bore some kinship to my own work, and I urged my agent to try its publisher: Berkley, a major imprint, actually, and part of Penguin. I was surprised we hadn't burned through them already. Auspiciously, my agent actually knew an editor there. The book had to be mailed twice because the Postal Service lost the first copy during a snow storm, a fact that nearly went undetected. And then, to no one's amazement more than mine, *Garrett in Wedlock* was accepted.

"We think we can grow him," the editor told my agent. Berkley mostly published chick lit (I hadn't bothered to learn this before), but as my new editor told me about the fiction marketplace in general, "It's all chick lit." How great, she said, that my second book was nearly done. How soon could I have a third?

"Books are the new magazines," my agent informed me. Who had the heart to tell my editor it had taken me ten years to write that first one?

At least she seemed to love *Adriane on the Edge.* "I'm dancing around my office," she said after reading it. And because all the stories in this one involved the same protagonist, Berkley could get away with simply calling it a novel, even though it wasn't a novel. It was that other thing. A *stovel*, as I like to call them.

"I just need to make the numbers work," my editor said about the contract. If they made it a two-book deal, and pushed enough of the advance till the later payouts . . . Mind you, we're talking about not a lot of money here. They'd need a deadline for the next book. I tried to pick the most distant date that wouldn't make their heads explode. But I'd failed to fully consider how Berkley was the same entity that, somewhere among its various sub-imprints, published Nora Roberts, author of 209 books and counting.

Pick an earlier date, I was told. The fine print of the contract specified this unwritten book was to be a standard novel, "not a novel-in-stories." They actually took the trouble to specify.

Since then, seven years have passed — Nora Roberts, by my imperfect reckoning, has published at least fifty novels in this time — and I have just recently finished mine, this one novel of ordinary length, which gave rise to many false starts and more than a million discarded words. In it, a beloved arts philanthropist appears to be stealing from the same museum he continues to support. An ambitious young journalist tries to prove it and, in the process, woo the beguiling curator who tipped him off in the first place. It's called *Museum of Trouble,* and I can finally look you in the eye and say I'm proud of this work.

But to Berkley, I am dead. I still recall the stunned response when the editor who'd taken over for my original one called to ask for a revised delivery date (we might have passed the initial deadline), and I proposed one that must have made her turn a few too many pages of her calendar. "It won't make sense to publish," I tried to explain, "until it's better than the first two books."

Do yourself a favor, should the situation ever arise, and never say anything remotely like that to an editor, unless you want to experience the most awkward silence of your career.

So: dead to Berkley I am, and the marketplace has only gotten tougher since my valiant agent sent to so many places *Garrett in Wedlock* — my first book. A sweet book, a good book. But not a novel.

No, my first real novel is still in manuscript, newly finished. Though who knows what improvements a wise editor may suggest, if and when I am lucky enough to find one? Which means, to be completely accurate, I am still writing my first novel, and may be for some time.

I know this from experience.

Paul Mandelbaum's fiction has appeared in *The Barcelona Review*, *DoubleTake*, *Glimmer Train Stories*, *Harvard Review*, and many other journals. He is the author of two novels-in-stories: *Garrett in Wedlock*, which won a James Michener-Copernicus Society of America Award and the 2005 Baltimore Book Festival Award for Fiction, and *Adriane on the Edge*. He also edited the anthologies *First Words: Earliest Writing from Favorite Contemporary Authors* and *12 Short Stories and Their Making*.

For more information, go to www.paulmandelbaum.com.

ASS BACKWARDS AND CLEARLY IMPOSSIBLE

MERRILL MARKOE

I got into writing books the same way it seems like I get in to everything: ass backwards. Even though looking back on my life, it certainly appears I was being raised to be a writer. But I think the reason it all happened ass backwards is because of one important detail: my mentor, also known as my mother, wanted to be a writer but never wrote. Obviously, if she had really felt writing was a desirable thing to be doing, she'd have been doing it herself. By example, she was teaching me to be a writer who didn't write.

What she did instead of write was go through all of my school homework with a red pencil and mark it up as though she were my copy editor. (Stet! Sp! New paragraph!) She was also very dedicated to having me adopt her preferred word choices, foregoing all slang from that period (e.g., cool, neat) in favor of "more descriptive words" such as "Delightful! Fantastic! Extraordinary!" And there was no explaining to her that it just felt wrong to stand with a group of my friends and tell them I thought their new clothes or haircuts were "Magnificent! Splendid!" By the time I graduated high school, I had been so thoroughly indoctrinated by her voice that whenever I tried to write, it felt as though she was doing the writing for me. Eventually, in order to make sure I was, in fact, the creative force behind my own work, I refocused my creative urges on the non-verbal. I became an art major.

By my mid-twenties, after a year spent teaching freshman painting and drawing at USC, art had begun to let me down as a supplier of income. But weirdly, despite never having taken a single writing class in college, somehow my instincts told me that writing was the area in which I had the most marketable skills. So I moved to Los Angeles, and began to submit writing samples to television. To my great surprise, I got hired almost immediately.

Next thing I knew, there I was with a budding career as a writer of TV comedy and film. That this had come to pass was such a shock to me, even as a TV writing career was unfolding, that it was impossible to think of myself as a real writer. After all, TV writing involved so much group collaboration. And writing jokes wasn't real writing, was it? Real writers got lost for days in the stacks of the library as they wandered in a scotch induced stupor, pondering arcane philosophies and the inscrutable issues of human existence. Real writers wrote books. Obviously, I could never do that . . . Now I began to feel more like a painter who wasn't painting, since the writer who wasn't writing kind of was.

Then one day someone offered me a chance to write a magazine piece. I decided to give it a try. That was the first time I felt the thrill of seeing my name in print, on a byline. I loved how it just sat there and didn't go anywhere instead of rolling past, just one more blur in a long list of names on a fast moving crawl timed out to match the length of a frolicsome theme song.

It never occurred to me that the magazine piece I'd written would lead to an offer from another magazine to write a monthly column. Even more unexpected was the phone call from a publisher a few years later, inquiring about collecting the columns in to a book of humor pieces. Not only did this mean that I would get paid a second time for work I had already finished, but . . . Wow. Somehow I had written a book! Collections of humorous essays were my favorite type of books back then. I read and re-read collections by Robert Benchley, Dorothy Parker, James Thurber, S. J. Perelman. It wasn't just exciting to think I'd be the author of my own collection, it was difficult to comprehend.

Over the next few years, I was allowed to publish two additional collections. But because it had all happened ass backwards, I still didn't see myself as a writer. It continued to be impossible for me to imagine sitting down to a blank piece of paper and causing a book to be born.

And then I was informed by my agent, via my publisher, that my collections of short pieces hadn't sold as well as they'd hoped. Publishers weren't interested in buying another collection from me. In fact, I would have to change categories if I wanted to sell another book at all.

Why?

Well, my agent explained, bookstores ordered books based on the number of your previous sales recorded on their computer. If your category was short humor pieces, and you only sold three of your last book in that store, then three was the maximum number they would order of any new book of humor pieces that you wrote. The only way to game this system was to change your category. Of the categories available to me, fiction was suggested as a possibility.

When my agent first said, "Why don't you try writing a novel?" it was as if she had said, "Would you be available to redesign the Hadron Super Collider?" It sounded inconceivable. The very idea of writing a single, first sentence that would somehow extend forward into an unknown horizon full of integrated subplots and fleshed out characters, all connected by written descriptions, was unfathomable.

So, after the idea was proposed to me, I did nothing at all about it for as long as I possibly could. I had no idea where to begin. When I wrote short humor pieces, I was able to envision them somewhere out in front of me, laid out in their entirety like a relief map. After that, it was just a matter of locating my target, aiming for it, and continuing to fire bullets until I hit something.

A novel seemed like a target so big I wouldn't know where to aim: a limitless, boundary-less universe containing many other galaxies. To say nothing of the fact that none of them could be reached until I found a way to burst through the frightening asteroid belt of radioactively intimidating names like Dostoevsky. Tolstoy. Faulkner. At least Joyce Carol Oates seemed, for one moment, a little bit more accessible because of those kooky glasses and that first name: Joyce. Of course, upon closer examination her forty novels and three Pulitzer nominations, as well as innumerable short stories, plays, novellas . . . Jeez. She was as terrifying as the rest of them.

So I continued to not begin my novel until one day, in the course of doing other things, I was booked to perform at a comedy show. Backstage I began a conversation with Moon Zappa as she and I were standing around, waiting to go on. She was in her early twenties. I was probably in my mid-forties.

"What have you been up to?" I think I must have asked her.

"I just published my first novel," she replied casually, as my jaw unhinged and hit me in the knees.

"How did you know how to write a novel?" I asked her. "I mean, I know how to assemble a bunch of short pieces into a book, but a novel . . . Where do you even begin?"

"Well," she said nonchalantly, "It's not really that different. What if you think of your novel as 15 chapters, 15 pages each?"

And with that off-handed, but brilliant, deconstructivist explanation, the massive fog bank began to lift around the prison on Alcatraz where the idea of a novel was locked in a solitary cell in my head. Using the Moon Zappa method of novel writing, a year later, I had finished a novel. By breaking the concept in small bite-sized pieces, I only had to create and control one chapter at a time. I could move forward.

This still did not make the day-to-day writing of a novel any easier for me. Connecting each chapter to the one before it and the one after it so that they were all heading in the same direction with the same velocity and shared internal elements of structure continued to be mind boggling. In fact, so formidable did I find the narrative process when I first began that I frequently had to imagine punching myself in the face, and then wrestling myself back down into a chair to make myself continue.

To be honest, everything about writing a novel continued to seem utterly impossible from the day I began to the day I finished. After years of writing screenplays, I resented having to stop and describe the frost on the goddamn window pane. Why couldn't I just say, "Cut to: frosty window," and let the art director and the cinematographer show everyone what I meant? Did I really have to bother finding words to explain "the impish twinkle" in someone's eye? What if I just put a pair of sunglasses on him and called it a day?

But I am basically a workaholic. So I kept at it.

I remember feeling like I might faint when I finally mailed a draft of it off to my editor. Obviously, I hadn't written "Crime and Punishment II." I had let everyone down. I still wasn't sure I was a real writer.

Now it's thirteen years later and I have finally come to accept that I am as real a writer as I would like to imagine myself to be. Apparently, I always could have written in any form I chose. I just had to learn how to overcome the voice of my mother who taught me how to be a writer who didn't write.

Unfortunately, understanding this now makes the challenge of writing a next book that much bigger. In my first novel I did the predictable thing just to facilitate forward movement: I wrote what I already knew. Now I realize that in my next novel, the challenge might be to write what I do not know yet, or what I would like to know.

Over time I've become a lot more realistic about the writing process and about the results. I've also learned how to block the neural pathways that cause me to be haunted by Dostoevsky. Ditto for Joyce Carol Oates. Except maybe when I'm picking out glasses.

Merrill Markoe is the author of four novels and four books of hopefully humorous essays, the most recent of which was "Cool, Calm & Contentious", published in 2012. In a previous life, she wrote for television, where she received five Emmys for her work on what was then called *Late Night with David Letterman*. She also makes theoretically funny videos, has hosted a radio show, done stand-up comedy and worked as an on camera reporter for local news. Merrill is currently finishing a play and at work on her fifth novel, which she would like you to think of as her first novel.

For more information, go to merrillmarkoe.com.

AUTHOR'S PREFACE TO
GARDEN STATE –
ANNOTATED EDITION[1]

Rick Moody

Jersey Sunsets[2]

My girlfriend and I were driving out into Jersey, out into the verdant part of the state. I don't remember where we

---

1 For some time now I have been considering writing and publishing an annotated edition of *Garden State,* my first novel. I have had this thought for a number of reasons. First, and foremost, *Garden State* is, in my view, a significantly ineffective first novel, and something that I have great trouble looking at or thinking about without wincing. An annotated edition of the novel might, at least, demonstrate that I know the limitations of this work, that I regret what I have done, and that I have come a long way. Second, I am a passionate believer in experiment, and, especially, in hybridized genres (neither of which belief you will find in the original *Garden State* at all), and an annotated edition of my first novel would allow me to furnish the book, this rather naked thing, with some of the decoration of its brethren, such as *Purple America, The Black Veil,* or *The Four Fingers of Death.* Third, there are interesting autobiographical details buried in the original *Garden State* — in fact, the autobiographical parallels with my own life would make the book more interesting if fleshed out. Fourth, I very much like the idea (as apparent in, e.g., *The Leaves of Grass,* by Whitman) that a book is never finished, and that different versions of the book might compete with one another, and I even like the legal gray area that this creates (i.e., would an

were going — to my sister's[3] house out near Peapack, to my brother's place in North Brunswick.[4] We were getting out of the corroded part of the state, where we lived. We'd been in Hoboken a year or so.[5] This was 1986. I played tapes in Lori's[6] car way too loud. I liked loud tapes besides.[7] That afternoon, I was playing a German cassette edition of *Crazy Rhythms* by the Feelies.[8] It was near dusk when we got swallowed into that tunnel, on Routes 1 and 9, on the way to the Pulaski Skyway. It's a long underpass, through which, at stroboscopic

---

annotated *Garden State* still be *Garden State,* or could I claim that it was a completely new work, if, for example, it was doubled in length — would the original contract still apply?). Also, I know a lot more about music now than I did then, and while *Garden State* has some of the seeds of the music writer who wrote *On Celestial Music,* the years have been kind to me and my relationship to music. I could certainly do a better job on the music part of the story than I might have before. Now, in the midst of this consideration on whether or not to annotate the novel, my agent, Melanie Jackson, noted the legal challenges, and I balked, on that basis – at least until a guy named Alan Watt contacted me to ask if I might write a few lines about the creation of my first novel for an anthology on this subject. I wrote back, "What if I annotated the preface?"

2 In *Garden State,* there are many references to DeLillo's *White Noise,* which was one of my favorite novels at the time. This preface was, as will be clearer later, written seven years after the novel was published (at the time I was working on *Purple America),* but still features a bit of the DeLillo preoccupation. These sunsets evoke the toxic clouds of DeLillo's masterpiece, though from a later vantage point.

3 My sister passed away in 1995. I was writing about a time when she was alive, but writing it when the wound of her death was still very fresh. It was in this time that I wrote the story "Demonology," too, so the emotionally vulnerable qualities in this preface are probably similar to the emotionally vulnerable qualities in that story.

4 When I was a kid growing up in Connecticut, I always looked down on New Jersey. And I considered people from New Jersey somehow less interesting.

intervals, the ambient light above illuminates the dingy unswept recesses of the roadway.[9] On this particular day, the tape was way up loud — it was "Raised Eyebrows" or "Crazy Rhythms" (with its long, jittery instrumental break), or the unsettling opening section of "The Boy with the Perpetual Nervousness."[10] Whichever, I was suddenly struck dumb by the arrangement of events, by light and sound and velocity, by the cant of life as I was rushing through it. In my twenties. In the flat part of New Jersey. I was angry and grateful at the

---

Consider the irony, then: in 1986, my sister, my brother, and I *all lived in New Jersey.*

5 I moved to Hoboken in spring of 1985, when I was asked to leave my dorm at Columbia for non-payment of rent. I had twenty-four hours to clear out. I put all my stuff in a U-Haul truck and parked it in an outdoor lot on the Upper West Side. My girlfriend and I found the apartment in Hoboken in a mad scramble lasting three days. It was cheap, and it had a good view of the Maxwell House factory.

6 She is still mad that I used her real name.

7 I'm not certain, at all, that what I liked then would be considered *loud* now. I liked Hüsker Dü a lot, and Pere Ubu, and the Minutemen, and The Feelies. Compared to Death Metal from Tampa, let's say, this all seems relatively benign on the *loudness* scale.

8 This whole preface, in my view, is taken up with the importance of The Feelies to *Garden State,* with how they are a shadow text in the whole (their lyrics, their sound, their approach, their reticence), but I still have never felt that I have dealt with the topic adequately, and I will try to bulk out what's here.

9 Still looks just like this, too, twenty-five years later.

10 "Perpetual Nervousness" is my favorite song on the first album, and I suppose it is not dishonest to say that part of the reason I like it is that I *was,* or believed myself to be, a boy with perpetual nervousness. There's a kind of vanity to this sort of self-identification, but my perpetual nervousness was so bad, in those days, that it was hard to get out of the orbit of self-absorption enough to have perspective.

same time, sad and overjoyed, and I didn't really know how to talk about it. Lori drove and didn't say anything.[11] The moment came and went. I was just starting *Garden State*.[12]

Writing School

The Feelies were a Jersey band, and I liked Jersey bands, especially Hoboken bands (Yo La Tengo, the dBs, the Silos, and others loosely associated with the region), because that's where I lived. That's why I started listening to them. I'd heard the Feelies before, though. I was a would-be punk[13] beginning in about 1979 and I heard their first album on WBCN[14] when

---

11 In *Garden State* and *The Ice Storm*, I often wrote about people who couldn't communicate, and whose conversations provided them with little relief. This is, I think, because I was myself not very good at talking to other people. I don't know, now, if this day, which I still remember, had anything to do with the beginning of *Garden State* or not. The beginnings of novels are, at least for me, historically obscure. They start long before you write the first sentence. And then they never end, even when you have already turned them in (and *this* is a good example — apparently I'm still working on *Garden State*).

12 One thing I didn't manage to describe the first time I wrote this preface is what I thought I was doing when I started my first novel. My recollection now from twenty-five years later is that I left graduate school thinking I would *never* write a novel, that I would always be a short story writer. I had contempt for all the writers trying to write books that would *sell*. I was only interested in things that had some kind of heavy emotional truth about them. I had the setting for *Garden State* first, because it was the setting I knew in Hoboken and Hudson County (though transported to a fictionalized Haledon), and all I needed was the people. I wrestled with who the people were for a long time, which is why it took two and a half years to write 212 pages. I suppose I broke my rule about never writing a novel

I was a sophomore in college. It had been my intention to stay in my dorm for the entire spring semester of that year. I took drugs a lot. I drank a lot. That was how I lived. It was also how I lived later when I was starting to write my first novel. Late seventies, early eighties.[15] The Feelies only performed on national holidays.[16] And between 1979, when I was in college, and 1986 when I started my novel, they were silent.[17]

I went to orientation and commencement at Brown in the same bad condition and then I went to get my MFA at Columbia. At which time I started drinking really heavily. Before I'd just drunk *a lot.* My girlfriend, Lorimer, was away in Paris, and I was getting into trouble in New York. One

---

because the people in the book were desperate to be heard. Or perhaps simply because I liked a challenge.

13 The self-mythologizing here is particularly hard to take, and I ask for your indulgence. I have no idea, really, what this line means, but I will say that I felt there was some sense of wanting to be part of the community of punk or new music or whatever you would call it. That was true in 1979, and true in 1986, and was even true in 1996 when I first wrote the preface, which means, I think that I was always someone outside with a nose pressed against the glass, wanting to be a part of whatever was new and exciting. This was especially true with music.

14 A really great Boston station that was noteworthy for breaking new rock and roll in those days.

15 All these sentence fragments! It really shows that, when writing the preface, I was able to recapture the fraggy grunge of my earlier prose style even though I was in the midst of developing the longer sentences that characterized my later work.

16 And they are reunited now, as you probably know, and are playing again, thirty or thirty-five years later, often on holidays.

17 Not entirely correct, but it makes for a good story!

night I was travelling from bar to bar with an undergraduate woman.[18] We went back to her apartment, and I remember in the midst of ill feeling and too-drunk-to-manage irritation there was this almost startlingly beautiful and sad song playing on her stereo.[19] It was on some college radio station. It turned out to be "On the Roof," from *The Good Earth,* the new record by the Feelies.

I heard the song on WNYU after that. Or was it WKCR? Don't remember. I heard it while I was trying to write and while I was drinking half-gallon bottles[20] of cheap bourbon that they dusted off for me at the package stores of Hoboken or on Upper Broadway. The opening snap of the snare drum from "On the Roof" always engendered in me this feeling of calm or melancholy. Maybe it was just the sound of real life, people in small towns getting in and out of regular, human predicaments.[21]

---

18 Now I think this undergraduate is a successful development person in the film world.

19 The question for the astute memoirist would be whether it was the song that was beautiful and sad or the situation that was beautiful and sad. Does the meaning inhere in the song, or is the song in some way the vessel for the situation? Was the song beautiful and sad because I couldn't be intimate with this red-headed undergraduate? I tend to think *yes,* that the song, regardless of its content, was about failure to be intimate with people, and that the reason *The Good Earth* seemed so great then was that its melancholy aspect was perfectly suited for my own mixed conversational abilities ("I don't talk much 'cuz it gets in the way," as Glenn Mercer sings). Writing the novel was one way to deal with all this, to try to get down on the page what I couldn't get down in life.

20 Sounds like a bad AA qualification in here.

21 With time, we always feel we have lost something precious, and here's the thing I have lost — conviction about what's *real.* At the time I wrote

Hollis, Queens

After graduate school things started to go really wrong.[22] I had psychiatric complaints. Panic attacks, phobias, bouts of depression. I had unexplained physical ailments too. Cuts and scrapes that wouldn't heal. Other difficulties too embarrassing to go into here.[23] I felt bad enough about all of this for it to be a problem. Then I was *asked to leave* by my girlfriend, and thereafter, in a real down spell, I committed myself to a psychiatric hospital in Queens, arguing naively that my sensitivity was becoming a real liability for me.[24] This did not turn out to be the name of my problem. I learned to play Scrabble in the hospital, and I learned, a little bit, to care about the welfare of other people. I got to like my

---

Garden State, and even when I was writing this preface seven years later, I thought I knew what was *real*, or that I could make some hierarchy of real, true things in the world, some of which were worthy of more attention than others. And now the world is more like a symphony in which all the instruments are clamoring for attention and none of them can be heard entirely. Conviction is a young man's game.

22 I think the danger for the sufferer with mental illness who tries to write about his troubles is that you are using the broken part of you to try to convey what was wrong. I can feel my anxiety here, as I can feel it in *Garden State*. When you are certain you are unable, in some fundamental way, to recognize exactly how things are, when you are gifted at concealing things from yourself, at least for a time, how do you know if you're telling *the truth?* To say that "things started to go really wrong" is to understate rather dramatically. And understatement is interesting, but inaccurate.

23 Sexual problems!

24 There are alcoholics who get really close to death from their drinking, whose livers fail, and so on. I was not one of those. I just couldn't function emotionally after a while.

fellow inmates on the adult ward.[25] Manic depressives, schizophrenics, bulimics, etc. I got to care about them. I think this is evident in *Garden State*. I was in the hospital in Hollis for twenty-nine days, just about the length of time spent in "Short Hills" by my protagonist, Lane.

After that, I lived for a time in a converted filling station on the bad side of Hoboken. A block from the projects. I was trying to get back to work. Feral dogs of the neighborhood, afflicted with fleas and mange, used to recline on my front step.[26] There were three different kinds of wood paneling in my gas station apartment, all in one room.[27] Occasionally, I went into the city, and took the F train to the end of the line, to Hollis, to look at the exterior of the hospital where I had done my time. Of *Garden State*, then, there existed maybe a chapter, and drafts of the next two. You can see in the finished product the fault line in me, in my life. Like the line a flood leaves after receding. In the book, the flood recedes between April and May.[28]

---

25 You know you are coming back from the worst part of addiction when you start to care about other people. And it's the only way I was ever going to finish *Garden State*, because I had to care about other people enough to *write* about other people.

26 The way I got out of the gas station apartment was simply to invite my parents to come for a visit. They took one look at the place and began conspiring to help me move elsewhere.

27 There's a passage about this in *The Black Veil* for those who are curious to know more.

28 This is partly to say how hard it was for me to finish this book. I was changing so fast as a writer, and changing so fast as a person. I would get down a chapter and almost immediately want to go back and start over. This happened several times. I also "lost" the manuscript a couple of times and

Town Hall

A couple of years later, in 1989, I finished my book. I'd been working at *America's largest publisher,*[29] Simon and Schuster, as a feckless[30] editorial assistant, and I had the manuscript of *Garden State* on my computer. When things slowed down at the office,[31] I'd turn on the computer and get going. When I moved to another publisher where the environment was less permissive,[32] I had to finish the book at nights, while doing my impersonation of a young media professional. One of the few things constant for me in the eighties was *The Good Earth,* that record by the Feelies. I'd go into tailspins, I'd neglect my job, I'd procrastinate on the book, but throughout it all I loved that record. I wore it out.[33]

---

had to retype it on the computer from earlier drafts or from memory. As if I didn't *want* to finish it somehow.

29 Sometimes I wonder exactly when my fondness for italics first began to take root. I can no longer pinpoint the precise date, but it had something to do with first using MS Word, and the ease of italicizing that came with that software package. I didn't have MS Word when I wrote *Garden State.* I had a Toshiba laptop where I saved everything onto "floppy" drives, and some word processing software that came with the machine, which no one after me probably ever used. But you can feel in the preface that I am beginning to figure out about the *glory* of italics.

30 This is a word I dislike now. And you know what else I dislike? Adjectives.

31 In retrospect, I think it's fair to say that things never slowed down in the office, I just had a boss who recognized that I was working on some other stuff. He was Allen Peacock, who was, at that time, one of the finer editors of literary fiction around. I was lucky to get to work with him at S&S, and he taught me a lot.

32 Farrar, Straus & Giroux, where I worked from 1988 to 1991.

33 Actually, as I might have already said, I had a lot of cassettes, and they wore out easily. I delayed getting CDs for a long time. I thought they were bourgeois.

I had theories about why the Feelies had been silent
for seven years between their first and second albums. One
theory had to do with personal travails of the sort I had gone
through.[34] I thought the Feelies — Glenn Mercer or Bill
Million, the songwriters — were, like me, recovering from
some melancholies, of the sort that Americans in suburban
municipalities everywhere seemed to have to go through:

Feeling so restless, so empty inside[35]

Plenty of chances and no one knows when

Over and over and over again

Needing somebody, needing some help

Slipping into something

Out of something else[36]

It didn't really matter if I was right about the genesis of
this wise and mumbled record or not[37] ("Glenn writes the

---

34 My friend Jonathan Lethem was a big fan of the Go-Betweens, and I think
whereas I had these theories about the Feelies, he had his about the Go-
Betweens. In each case, the interpretations were somewhat solipsistic.
Wherever we looked we found our own predicaments and inclinations,
which is the vanity of youth.

35 Now what appears to be the case about Glenn Mercer's lyrics is that they
are so oblique that it is *easy* to project meanings onto them. The lines I like
best (like: "Late at night/distant voices/burning cars/out on the highway")
are those that are less so. But it's probably that balance between meaning
and abstraction that made *The Good Earth* great. And which made it a good
companion for me and my book.

36 I did in fact get permission to quote from these lyrics at the time I wrote this
preface. I sent Bill Million a FedEx package, care of the Feelies publishing
company, which turned out to be located at Bill's house, and, he told me,
the FedEx guys woke him up. Other than that, he was pretty amiable,
and explained that my dates were all wrong, and it couldn't possibly have
happened the way I said.

lyrics," Bill Million once said, "and we don't ask him what they mean"). For *Garden State,* it only mattered what I *believed* was true. Thus, the novel ended up located in Haledon, New Jersey, where the Feelies lived (and live still), not in Hoboken, where I lived. Music, see, exerted a considerable influence on what I was doing.[38] Music taught me a lot of whatever I know about prose, about the way that prose should sound. *The Good Earth. New Day Rising. Dub Housing. Let It Be.*[39] *Astral Weeks.*[40]

After I finished *Garden State,* it was rejected by every publisher in New York.[41] Bill Henderson, who eventually published the Pushcart Press edition, fished the manuscript out of some stack of prize nominees mainly because he took me for some sort of crypto-religious writer.[42]

After the book was accepted, I got fired from my job, I

---

37 And it's fortunate that it didn't matter, because I don't think my interpretation had much merit.

38 Here's where you can make out the music columnist waiting to happen.

39 By the Replacements, not the Beatles.

40 This is the one thing that is not like the other things in the set. I was completely obsessed with this album in the late eighties, and it eclipsed, in a way, my total saturation with indie rock. *Astral Weeks* is all about the lyrics, and about the unlikely fact that a twenty-three-year-old guy could have written "Sweet Thing" or "Madame George" with just what he knew then.

41 It was, it should be said, exceedingly hard to be a young editor going to a lot of book parties and events, seeing a lot of people who had just or were about to reject your manuscript. Even my boss at FSG rejected it, saying "It's too hermetic." By which I think he meant: too depressing. And from this vantage point I can hardly quarrel.

42 Maybe he was right, if by religious you mean writing with a certain kind of moral indignation.

fell in love, I fell out of love. All of that.

Meanwhile, I decided that I wanted the Feelies to *give me a blurb for the jacket of the book.* Through a friend in the record business, I made contact with their manager. My record business pal and I got backstage passes for what turned out to be just about the last Feelies concert ever.[43] Town Hall, NYC, May 1991. The show was pretty good.[44] Afterward, we went backstage to meet them.

I left my manuscript with Brenda, the bass player.[45] Later, I sent another copy to Bill Million.[46] I'm pretty certain the Feelies never read it. Or perhaps they just didn't like it.[47] The important point for this introduction is that they were smart, articulate people; they gave me lectures on union organizing in Haledon and on William Carlos Williams's epic poem, *Paterson* — set in the industrial city next to Haledon. But

---

43 At least until they started having the reunion concerts.

44 They jumped around a lot at the end. I think they played "Sedan Delivery" and "She Said, She Said," along with many originals.

45 Brenda Sauter, a very amazing and melodic bass player.

46 By the way, one reason the Feelies stopped playing for a long time is that Bill Million got a job working in IT at Disney World. He moved to Florida. I think he still lives there, actually, and commutes north for gigs.

47 I got a chance to interview them a few years ago in the midst of their reunion, and it's true that they are not easy guys to talk to. Glenn just doesn't really talk at all and routinely leaves longer conversational gaps than other mortals would tolerate. Bill is acerbic and hilarious, but also somewhat laconic, and he doesn't necessarily leap in to help with the long conversational silences. They seemed to know who I was and to remember that we had had some interaction years back, but I am not sure that they are people who read what is written about them much. They operated according to some Feelies hive brain where all the decisions are made fairly intuitively, without the need for chatter. I admire this approach.

they looked kind of spooked when I made clear that I wanted them to *write a couple of sentences about my book.* These were guys who happened to make really great records. Guys from the suburbs, like I was from the suburbs. They had day jobs. They were honest people. Fan worship just didn't make sense to them. And it didn't really make sense to me anymore either. I was growing up a little.[48]

Brooklyn

My hypothesis is that a period of my life came to its conclusion when I finished *Garden State.* The Feelies broke up. I went freelance. I moved out of Hoboken. Wrote another book. Two more since.[49] When I look back at this novel — and I don't very often — it looks to me like the work of a particularly troubled teenaged sibling. A proto-slacker. He's sloppy, pretentious, not very good on follow-through, but sympathies matter to him.[50] And that's good.

---

48 Probably wishful thinking here.

49 Now eight or nine since *Garden State,* depending on how you count.

50 The whole period in which I wrote *Garden State* now looks to me like a big, black hematoma. It looks like a half-decade or so of pain. Maybe this is what first novels are like. I'm sure there are writers out there who just effortlessly flush out a great first novel — *it was just right there under the shrub! I picked it up and mailed it to ICM!* But I was not one of those. Finishing the book, living through what I lived through to finish the book, scarred me. And I'm not overstating the case. Whether the mental illness caused the book, or the book caused the mental illness, I do not know, but I know that the two were coincident and that a lot of the delusional thinking that I might have pinned on drinking and drugs was also delusional thinking that accompanied the work on this book well after I cleaned up. I think what it

I don't think I've ever again been able to write anything as naked as this book you have before you.[51] In this light, I can understand the proposition put forth by a vocal minority: that *Garden State* is my best novel.[52] I don't agree, but I can understand in this way what it's like to be judged by the feelings of your younger incarnation, like Elvis Costello sometimes is. Or like the Feelies are. *Garden State* tried to delineate a place and time and a mood that a lot of people seemed to embrace a few years later. After Richard Linklater's first movie,[53] after *Nevermind.* It's seven years since I finished this book.[54] I hope I never have to live that way again:

---

took for me to be more than a minor player, more than just a back-office line editor who had some pretensions about writing, was a journey into a rather isolated and estranged place. The result, alas, was not a good first novel, but it was good enough to permit me to write a second. And the second novel actually did pretty well. (That's another story.)

51 By "naked" I think what I meant was without guile. Defenseless.

52 Actually, I know of only one person who still believes this. I don't think anyone really attends to *Garden State* now, except when there's no other book of mine left on the merch table after readings. It should be obvious that this is the least artful thing I've ever written. I don't want to prevent you from reading this book, but I want you to know the context.

53 Pavement would be a good analogy, too. Or the Silver Jews. Or Hal Hartley's early films.

54 And now it's been twenty-three years or so. I remember a professor at Columbia, when I was getting my degree there, saying that any book that lasted ten years in print had accomplished something. There is no reason this book is still in print, except that they sell a few more every time a new book comes out. I can barely recognize the aesthetic impulses here. I no longer believe a story can be told in a linear fashion, really, and I think naturalism is a spent literary force. And yet here is my younger self. *Ecce puer.*

You know what the others know —
Seven years, way too long.
Talk about the old fun,
People never listen hard.
I can't stay, it's got to be that way . . .[55]

— Rick Moody,
October 1996[56]

Rick Moody is the author of five novels, including *The Ice Storm* and *The Four Fingers of Death*; three collections of stories; a memoir entitled *The Black Veil,* and, most recently, a volume of essays, *On Celestial Music.* He plays and sings in The Wingdale Community Singers, and writes music criticism for *The Rumpus* (www.therumpus.net).
For more information, go to
www.hachettebookgroup.com/features/moody/.

---

55 By the way, there's a new Feelies album out, as of 2011, called *Here Before.* (And I reviewed it here: http://therumpus.net/2011/09/swinging-modern-sounds-31-reunion-fever/)

56 Rick Moody, September 2012

IN THE TRADITION

DAVE NEWMAN

I did what I always did when I wanted to write but couldn't: I picked up a Richard Brautigan novel and took it to bed. The novel was called *So the Wind Won't Blow It All Away*. It starts like this: "I didn't know that afternoon that the ground was waiting to become another grave in just a few short days." I love the drama in that sentence but I love the simple language, too. The next sentence in the novel is even better but you should see that one for yourself.

I read the first couple of chapters then stopped. It was late afternoon. I was on my back, dreaming a scene for the novel I'd been working on.

Richard Brautigan wrote in the mornings, probably hungover, then spent his afternoons watching B-movies. He thought the monsters on the screen, the blobs and UFOs, cleared his head for an evening back at his typewriter.

My head filled with images, too many. I imagined schoolteachers and bar owners and taxi drivers, and those were just the minor characters. Everyone wanted to be in my novel until I put them in my novel then everyone moved awkwardly and tried to escape.

This was 1998. I lived in a three-room apartment in Hollsopple, Pennsylvania, a tiny town west of Johnstown and east of Pittsburgh. Hollsopple was basically a farm that grew Mennonites and people who voted Republican. The Post Office kept odd hours. Pumpkins filled the rolling fields. The craft stores sold mailboxes shaped like barns and taverns. After months of negotiations, the local gay bar now housed a church in its basement. Before that, the Christians had lined up outside the bar with picket signs and marched around a barrel filled with fire, singing Christian songs and shouting Christian slogans. Now there appeared to be a harmony, or at least a quietude, and gay people now arrived for a drink and headed inside without having to stand up to an angry mob.

Weirdness, genuine American weirdness, emerged like flags going up poles on the Fourth of July, and Hollsopple lived every day like a patriotic holiday. Neighbors shot deer in their backyards. You could trout fish anywhere. Burger King bags littered the woods by the main road like fast food berries in trees.

My reality, Hollsopple, often felt like a dream, and that's how Richard Brautigan wrote. He didn't take fast cars to Vegas or contemplate World War II. He drank wine in the park with hobos and bums and ate free sandwiches at the mission. Anyone could do war and Vegas. Hobos and bums and free sandwiches were the real hardships. Death was a casual thing, not a tragedy. Brautigan showed me that. So I went to the gay bar a couple times even though I wasn't gay. I talked to the picketers one night even though I thought a gay bar in a farm community was a good idea. I warmed my hands over the fire in the barrel and drank a can of Schafer beer.

I knew a lot about Richard Brautigan: his writer friends, his drinking habits, his girlfriends and wives, the apartments in San Francisco, the ranch in Montana, the trips to Japan. I knew he liked guns and he'd once shot up his own kitchen clock. I thought knowing his life would help me understand his imagination and knowing his imagination would help expand my own. Richard Brautigan said, "Because you always have a clock strapped to your body, it's natural that I should think of you as the correct time." I didn't have a clock strapped to my body. I didn't know the correct time. I was beginning to doubt I'd ever be a writer.

Richard Brautigan existed in a world where language and experience were inseparable. Going to the grocery store was enough to launch a brilliant metaphor. Anything more felt like a moon landing. Brautigan wrote what is still the best poem ever about a blowjob.

I don't remember how I learned so much about Richard Brautigan back in 1998. Internet was available but I didn't have it. I didn't have cable. My TV had bunny ears. My radio only played if I balanced it on a window ledge. I'd had a job as a furniture store manager but I'd lost it. I had a little bit of money saved and I could collect unemployment. All I wanted was to be a writer with a book.

My novel narrated the story of a guy and his fat friend. There was a woman, too. She owned a pharmacy. She was a pill addict. I knew a woman like that. I knew the guy and the fat friend. But when I wrote them they all looked cartoonish and melodramatic.

Richard Brautigan wrote simple, clean sentences. His characters were tiny in their flaws and in their successes, which is to say his characters felt real.

I wanted my characters to be real. They were real. They existed and had names and birthdays. But when I moved them from my world into my imagination and out onto the page they reappeared as clumsy, obnoxious blobs.

I looked at the Richard Brautigan novel. It didn't make sense that I should be able to read such an interesting book so many times and yet not be able to write anything great myself.

So the Wind Won't Blow It All Away is a novel told in reverse. It's the story of a grown man looking back on the day he bought bullets instead of a hamburger. It's a brilliant book. The narrative addicts the reader like a narcotic. The images delight. The voice is as clear as a bartender asking if you'd like another or a bouncer telling you to go home.

Brautigan has a line somewhere: "All of us have a place in history. Mine is clouds." Knowing your place in history is important if you're going to become a writer. I knew that but I still couldn't find my place. I was not a cloud. I was not even a furniture store manager anymore. I was twenty-eight years old. I owed fifty grand in student loans. If I didn't become a writer soon, I assumed it would never happen. Nobody, I believed, published their first book after thirty.

Brautigan published his first chapbook at twenty-three. He published his first novel, *A Confederate General in Big Sur*, when he was twenty-nine.

What had I done?

I'd published forty or so poems and a handful of stories in literary magazines and journals. I'd been in the *Wormwood Review* with Charles Bukowski. I'd been paid 500 dollars for a short story by a New York magazine. I'd been drunk a few times with Ed Ochester, one of my favorite poets, and I regularly corresponded with Gerald Locklin, a brilliant poet who had corresponded and drank with Charles Bukowski. I'd been offered a job making thirty-eight grand a year, a huge sum of money for me (then and now), and I'd turned it down because I didn't think I could sell industrial parts all day and come home and still be an artist at night.

When I write that now, the publications and the friendships and the dedication to living as a writer, it all sounds brilliant, but it wasn't brilliant at all. It was the opposite of brilliant. I'd been drunk with Ed Ochester when I was his student, paying tuition, and lots of other students, some not paying tuition but on scholarship, were drunk with Ed Ochester, too. Gerald Locklin, after four decades in the small press, taught four classes a semester at a state school in California and still struggled to reach a broader audience. Charles Bukowski was dead.

I went back to my novel.

I went back to Richard Brautigan.

If I would have known that I wouldn't publish my first novel for almost a dozen more years, I'm not sure I would have kept on. I might have gone back to the company that offered me thirty-eight grand and said, "Please," and, "I'll sell anything."

Back in my apartment, I went to sleep and woke up and

went back to my novel then back to Richard Brautigan then back to sleep. It was endless. Writing had never been so little fun, so lacking in vision and spirituality. The whole thing was a fucking drag.

Two months before this, I'd written a query (or what I'd imagined a query to be; I'd never seen one) and shipped it off with some stories to 7 Stories Press. The publisher there, Dan Simon, said he liked the stories and asked to see my novel. I guess I'd mentioned I had a novel, but what I had were drafts of novels, most unfinished, all pretty bad. Now I was working frantically, as if I had a publishing contract and not a letter that said, basically, "Yeah, okay."

7 Stories was (is) a great press. Dan Simon started it to reissue the novels of Nelsen Algren. Nelsen Algren created a character, Railroad Shorty, that inspired Richard Brautigan to create a character, Trout Fishing in America Shorty. All I needed to do to continue on that train with those guests was write a novel, or revise a novel, into a good book, because what I had written was not good, certainly not good enough to be on 7 Stories Press and share space with my heroes.

Now I was stuck. I'd been up all morning. I'd written. I'd gone running. I'd written again. It was dinnertime, and I didn't have another thing to say. Richard Brautigan couldn't save me. Nelson Algren couldn't save me. I thought 7 Stories Press would save me but thinking about 7 Stories press and that pressure made me feel worse.

I had twenty pages completed. My goal for the day had been thirty pages. The math was obvious but I couldn't add anything to the manuscript. I was bored. My characters were bored. My sentences ran as long and winding as rivers and had about as much to say. If I didn't finish and publish a novel in the next four months, my money would be gone, and I'd have to do what I'd promised myself I'd do: become a truck driver and give up on all those things I imagined decent writers having — recognition, a job at a small college, a home that didn't roll on eighteen wheels.

So I focused on the four months. I had a stack of paper covered in words, what I would have called a solid draft. But it was really a 300-page rant about bad jobs and worse friends, terrible sex and prescription drugs. I was 150 pages into the revision, but when I went past that, I'd get confused and disappointed and have to revise the first 150 pages. This had happened five or six times and I was afraid it was about to happen again.

To get my pages, I was willing to try anything: B-Movies, diet pills, a box of Little Debbie cakes. I would have turned over and fucked the cover of *So the Wind Won't Blow It All Away* if I thought it would have helped, but of course fucking a pile of bound pages is no more inspiring than pressing the cover of the book to my forehead and demanding Brautigan's images work their way into my brain through osmosis. Some days, I wrote with the window open. Other days, I wrote with the heater on. A month before this, I'd tried writing on dope but before I could form a thought and translate that thought into words, I puked in the garbage can. The rest of the day I spent in the bathroom, throwing up and sleeping under the toilet, feeling relieved I wasn't writing.

Time, for writers, is measured in two things: the amount

of words we read and the amount of words we write. I hadn't done enough of either.

I burned more candles. I tried caffeine and valium. I moved my word processor from my bedroom to my living room which was also my kitchen. I moved it back.

What I should have done was write my novel straight through then I should have written some poems then another novel then some more poems then some stories and so on.

No one, not one of my writer friends and certainly none of my teachers, had told me it was so simple. You read and write until you have a book you're proud of, then someone publishes that book. If they don't publish that book, you write another one.

I finished rereading *So the Wind Won't Blow It All Away* that afternoon. Over drawn-out and confused days, I reread the rest of Richard Brautigan's books as I worked on and finished my own novel, a 307-page stack of paper inked up with sentences I imagined to be true. The whole process took a month, and it was great — the finishing, not the novel.

Then I got terrifically shitfaced drunk and fucked a woman I could barely stand. I sent my novel off to 7 Stories Press and knew that I was about to become famous, if not famous then celebrated, if not celebrated then at least published. I'd have a book to put on my shelf. If someone asked, I could show them.

When 7 Stories Press didn't get back to me, I signed up to become a long-haul trucker.

Being a trucker was awful.

It was not a job teaching college.

It was not being a famous, semi-famous, or an underground writer.

Being a trucker was not the job I'd paid fifty thousand dollars to go to college to become. Being a truck driver was not my vocation. I started to imagine I'd never publish a book, the kind of reverse fantasy that kills young artists.

And yet I kept writing.

I was in Montana one day, picking up a load at a warehouse, and I thought: Richard Brautigan. Rivers and trees lined the warehouse, I was tired, and my only thought was: Richard Brautigan. It was pure and simple and not connected to anything but the man and the books he wrote. The warehouse guys unloaded my truck. I drove on. Richard Brautigan, I thought. It was what I wanted to do with my life, think thoughts like Richard Brautigan and Nelson Algren, Ed Ochester and Gerald Locklin, Charles Bukowski. Nothing else came close to those thoughts.

Other things happened to me during my time as a truck driver, some fun, some terrible, some both, but every day I wrote at least one poem. When I dead-headed home to my apartment, I worked on my novel. I wrote stories then started another novel then wrote more poems. I did this for years. I do it now.

Working — reading and writing — matter more than publishing.

I know that now but forget it still.

If you want to be a cloud, be Richard Brautigan.

If you want to be a writer, write.

Dave Newman is the author of the novels *Raymond Carver Will Not Raise Our Children* (Writers Tribe Books, 2012) and *Please Don't Shoot Anyone Tonight* (World Parade Books, 2010). He lives in Western Pennsylvania with his wife, the writer Lori Jakiela, and their two children.

For more information, go to
www.davenewmanwritesbooks.com.

WHEN THE HALF-LISTENING MEET THE HALF-TRUTHFUL: TEN MEDITATIONS ON WRITING THE SHORT STORY COLLECTION

Mary Otis

When I first began to write, I thought, if I ever publish a single short story, I will die a happy woman. The form is mysterious and demanding, and most of the time I feel like I'm working with a kind of emotional divining rod, waiting to be pulled toward the small detail or single line that yanks me into a story. When this occurs, it feels urgent; it feels like I have no say in the matter. Then there's the permission part. I never worry while I'm actually writing, but I worry plenty once I'm finished. *Well, I've really gone and done it now* runs through my mind on a ceaseless ticker tape.

I once taught a writing class for teenagers. At the end of the first week, a student came up to me, a boy who hadn't uttered a word in class, and said, "I tend to write about vulgar, violent things. And alcoholics. Is that a problem?" And there you have it. What you want to write about is what you need to write about, and you can no more change that than will your eyes to change color.

When my short story collection, *Yes, Yes, Cherries* was bought,
I had a partial manuscript that consisted of six or seven
published stories. My editor, Lee Montgomery at Tin House,
advised me to write three more. I was simultaneously thrilled
and stunned, as if I'd been slightly electrocuted. I never
expected to have my collection bought before it was finished.
Now all I had to do was write those three stories.

The next day, my landlord informed me I would need
to move. I lived in a cottage on a beautiful estate in Los
Feliz, and it was up for sale. A few days later, I came home
to find prospective buyers in my apartment. One of them
was standing in my kitchen drinking a blue Super Slurpee,
stroking his beard, absently reading my story manuscript,
which was laid out on the counter. The landlord said, "Oh,
here's the writer now," as if they had been expecting me all
along. I needed to get out of there.

A month went by. I couldn't find a place. I still needed to
write three stories. Then came the sandblasting of the exterior
of my cottage. Then came the chain saws and the removal of
an oak tree that leaned against my roof like a drunk at the
bar. Then came the painters and a strange, overly cheerful
yellow color. The color seemed to say: if you live in this house,
you will awake each morning and shout, "How Up I Am!"

Then the house sold. Then I began to panic. Out of sheer
anxiety I began to drive the freeways at night, a habit I still
indulge when distress calls. My boyfriend calls this "getting

the Didions" — referencing the character Maria in *Play It As It Lays*, who aimlessly drives Los Angeles highways. I basically drove the next story, "Unstruck" into being — late at night, or early in the morning, thinking and motoring, stopping from time to time to write notes in a parking lot. This story would not sit still, and the only way I could catch it seemed to be to stay in motion myself.

During the editing process, my editor and I discussed linking some of the already published stories. A few of them very naturally went together because they were essentially based on the same character. I tried and tried to link the others, but it was like taking people from six different parties, locking them in a room, and insisting that they talk to each other. High school reunions, long lost family connections, byzantine and nutty coincidences, I tried them all. In the end, the ones that organically linked stayed together, and the others remained separate. I once heard that souls travel in packs, and I think characters do, too. They just don't necessarily all want to be in the same story.

When I began writing my collection, before I had published much, I attended a summer writing conference. On the first day, the teacher gave us an exercise. We were to recall one of the most humiliating times of our lives and bring it to class the next day. Then we would tell the group the story in ten minutes or less. Later in the week, each of us would work the memory into a fictional story. I immediately thought of something, but rather than write about it, I spent every waking minute before class trying to make up a fictional most humiliating moment, because I really didn't feel like sharing the actual memory with a bunch of people I'd just met.

It was a few minutes before class when the best I'd come up with was a concocted memory of being lost in a park. So, when it came my turn to tell the most humiliating day story, I ended up telling the actual story that had to do with a troubled period in my life, and which prior to that point simply seemed too stupid and embarrassing to incorporate in any kind of story, ever. But in the end, I told the class about the time I went to a drunk therapist, and that became the basis for the story "Stones," which was one of the first stories I ever had published. So, you never know when a bad time in your life can be put to good use in a story, or as the writer, Steve Almond, calls it, "wringing beauty from the neck of shame."

I once met a woman who wanted to be a writer. She said she'd start as soon as she found the right chair. I've never fallen prey to that particular avoidance, but during the assembly of my collection, there were times that I stopped writing for a while, sometimes directly after I'd had a story published. I thought I would write when I was less worried about whatever it was

I was worried about (cue the *I've really done it now* music). I would write when I felt calmer or more confident, when I had felt like a person who had something of great value to say. A storm of doubt would overtake me, and the next thing I knew I'd spent my writing time organizing the silverware drawer.

But in the end, I couldn't wait. I had those three stories to write. And so I did. They say action is the antidote to anxiety. In the end, I had to think like a postal carrier and take to heart that motto: *Neither rain, nor snow, nor sleet shall keep a postman from his appointed rounds.* Except the rounds were my writing work, and I had to get my seat in the chair.

Writing a story seems to be about intention and availability — not only to the story itself, but availability to daily life that sneaks in around the side and gets in there, too. One day I was shopping in Ralphs on Sunset Boulevard, and a man asked me how I was doing. I told him I was fine. He said, "Me, I just got out of jail." This went directly into a short story and was exactly what needed to come out of the mouth of a character I was writing. The trick is that you never know where you will find what, so I try to dwell in a place of possibility, and often the world feels like it's leaning in, conspiring with me to write the story.

Not long before my collection was published, I was on a

plane, and the woman sitting next to me asked me what I did. I told her and she asked me what my book was about. And here's where I clutched, and often do, when someone asks me what the stories are about. Basically all I have to do is repeat what's on the jacket flap of my book. But instead I find myself trying to explain the emotional geography of my stories, my hopes for the capture and illumination of small significant moments in life.

Frequently, when I begin a story, I give myself a secret suggestion, something that wouldn't mean anything to anyone but me. This "clue" usually ends up informing a story in a way I never would have expected. The image of a piece of embroidery comes to mind — how it looks like a tangled mess on the back but makes sense on the front. And the difficulty comes in trying to tell somebody about the back of the embroidery. On that plane ride, I decided that if I couldn't summarize my stories in a couple of sentences, I needed to come up with a simple phrase — a kind of catchall for the human condition.

A couple of weeks later, I was at a book signing. I was reading from *Yes, Yes, Cherries*, and during the last paragraph a man stormed into the bookstore. When I finished he came up to me and said, "So what is this book about?"

"Well," I said, "It's about people facing challenges, people trying to change."

The man looked like he'd eaten a spoonful of mustard.

"You know, the regular," I said.

The man squinted his eyes at me. "What??" he shouted.

I tried again. "Well, you know . . . it's about (and here

I had the horrible and familiar sinking feeling of being unable to articulate a single thought about a book I spent five years writing) . . . it's about doubt and fear and overcoming limitations."

The man suddenly lit up. "Oh. I get it!" He picked up my book, flipped it over, tapped his index finger on the cover, and said, "It's like *Bridge Over the River Kwai!*"

Exactly.

The hardest thing and the best thing about writing the short story collection was committing to a daily appointment with my subconscious. I'm invested in not only how a story is told but in what shakes and rumbles beneath it — the emotional engine.

When I was young, I loved to fall asleep listening to the adults talking late into the night. Urgent gossip. Amazing confessions. Things I wasn't supposed to hear. I was an expert fake sleeper. But as the hour grew late, I would begin to drift off while simultaneously the adult conversations and claims heated up, became wilder. Fiercely, I tried to hold on, but my listening strength seemed to diminish in equal proportion to the exaggeration of the tale — when the half-listening meet the half-truthful. I was kind of listening, they were kind of telling the truth, and it all mixed into some wonderful tangle of memory I wasn't sure of the next day — something I would vow to remember, inevitably forget, and immediately begin to embellish. It was a sort of willful enchantment, and my first encounter with the homeland of fiction. The trick is to stay in that place forever.

Every time I write a short story, I don't know how to do it. This doesn't seem to get better, but I take great heart from a quote by the poet, Paul Valery: *There is in you that which is beyond you.*

Mary Otis is an award-winning writer whose short story collection *Yes, Yes, Cherries* was published by Tin House Books. She has had stories and essays published in Best New American Voices (Harcourt), *Los Angeles Times*, *Tin House*, *Electric Literature*, *Berkeley Literary Journal*, *Alaska Quarterly Review*, *Cincinnati Review*, *Santa Monica Review*, *The Rumpus*, and *Los Angeles Review of Books*. Her writing has been anthologized in *Do Me: Tales of Sex and Love* (Tin House) and *Woof: Fiction Writers on Dogs* (Viking). Her story "Pilgrim Girl" received an honorable mention for a Pushcart Prize, and her story "Unstruck" was named a Distinguished Story of the Year in the Best American Short Stories. She is a Walter Dakin Fellow, and in 2010 was a literary advisor in The Mark Program created by PEN. Originally from the Boston area, Mary is a fiction professor in the UC Riverside Low-Residency MFA Program where she is part of the core faculty. She is currently at work on a novel.

For more information, go to <u>www.maryotis.com</u>.

GNAWING THE BONE

Leslie Schwartz

*"Pursue, keep up with, circle round and round your life . . .
Know your own bone: gnaw at it, bury it, unearth it, and gnaw
at it still"*

— Thoreau,
as quoted in Annie Dillard's *The Writing Life*

Writing my first novel, *Jumping the Green* (Simon & Schuster, 1999), was a struggle between the knowledge that I had a story to tell, and the fear that I would not be honest in the telling. I knew intuitively when I was being a phony. I could feel the twinge in my stomach. The words ringing in my ears: *You aren't being true.*

I often found this idea of truth-telling to be one of my biggest hurdles. It wasn't that I needed to get "the facts" straight. After all, I was writing a novel. No, the truth meant telling a story that had meaning for me, even if *they* didn't like it.

Who are *they*? Mom and Dad. Brothers. Agents. Friends. Publishers. Anyone who had the power to convince me that what I was doing was either a waste of time or irrelevant. Why, people asked me, would I write a novel — spend all that time on something — and not get paid for it?

There was no way to answer that question. Relevancy, for me, lay simply in the act of writing. The joy I felt when I could string a couple of sentences together felt almost holy. It was my secret.

And therein lay the struggle. If I were to have this secret, I would have to also be honest, because by its very nature, a secret is the truth. How could I write without delving into the darkness, the power of my character to tell a story I held dearly, but was fearful of revealing?

The truth is, I often was incapable of summoning up the courage. Because rigorous honesty requires immense bravery, and there were days when my fortitude crumbled in the face of the story I was telling. *Jumping the Green* is a dark book, and a little "off the grid." No Oprah Book Club selection for sure. And I knew that though it was fiction, there was some small part of me in it as well. That the baring of these little truths would be hurtful to the people I loved who would read it was self-evident.

I also had the problem of having to pay the mortgage. I was working full time and had little time to write. So what I would do was type up the work my bosses wanted me to type, spreadsheets, letters, proposals, but really I'd switch screens and work on my novel. If they walked by, I'd quickly switch screens again. Though they soon figured it out, they said they didn't mind, and for that I've always been grateful. One problem solved.

But there still remained the problem of being truthful to myself as a writer, and by extension to my characters and the story. I was never one to gather up how-to writing books filled with prompts and advice. I was not interested in getting an MFA, though eventually I did acquire my MFA. At the time, I just wanted to write.

Then one day, it occurred to me: why bother writing at all if you aren't going to give it your all. I also accepted the idea that maybe fearlessness was a process, not something that just settled in and stayed. It was a daily conquering. I had to purposefully remove the critics from my shoulders, myself most especially, and all the others, real or imagined, on a daily basis.

Certainly writers acquire bizarre or mystical habits. I once read that John Cheever walked to his office every day in a business suit and then stripped down to write in his underwear. And Isabelle Allende very famously lights candles and incense to keep the "spirits and the muses" coming.

But I have never been one for magic or superstitions. I decided that fearlessness and courage were a practice and as such required a practical degree of habit and commitment. I turned down party invitations. I didn't return phone calls. I barely saw my husband. Every morning I walked my dog through Elysian Park, pen and pad in hand and jotted down what I would write that day so that I would not have to face the horror of an empty screen. And I told myself I had to write an hour a day. Word count could be a bummer — if I didn't meet a prescribed word count I would feel like I'd failed. Outcomes were the death-knell. Never think about outcomes, I told myself. And my constant refrain was this: write whatever the hell you want, it's not cast in stone.

I stuck to this regimen. And in so doing, I began to write more freely. I am not sure when it happened, but I am guessing that at some point when the routine kicked in, I no longer cared what anyone would think about this crazy character I was creating and the mess she had made of her life, much of it dizzyingly sexual and alcohol-fueled. It was my story to tell. And if you didn't like it, well then, tough.

And I really did come to feel that way. Then I had the good fortune of being accepted for a six-week residency at Hedgebrook, a writer's colony on Whidbey Island in Washington. Being in the company of other writers, and struggling with the same issues was heavenly. I had spent so much time alone, that my doubts had doubts. But here I was thrust into the company of other writers who also spoke about truth and honesty in writing. Since then, I have never attempted to write anything without at least one or two good readers who won't kowtow to me, but will give it to me straight so I might write the best book possible.

Eventually, I found freedom from my worries about finding "the truth." I understood that when I was able to find *my own* truth, the novel would certainly speak to some people. And it did to many people who read it. For others it was roundly hated, if Amazon reviews are to be taken seriously. But that didn't matter. What mattered was the realization that it would have been the death knell for my book had I tried to write it from some agenda, to proselytize an idea or a political position or any position for that matter.

Courage came from understanding my character and being true to her and to her incredible jeopardy and her journey out of her downward spiral. By putting the emphasis on her and her dilemma, I eventually got out of my own way.

A week before he died, Paul Monette was asked by writer Terri Jentz for the single piece of advice he could give her about writing her own story. He replied that every day he sat down to work, he would ask himself to write more honestly than he had the day before.

That's the burden and the luxury of writing your first novel: interrogating the truth each and every day you write.

Leslie Schwartz is the author of *Jumping the Green,* which won the James Jones Literary Society Award for Best First Novel and *Angels Crest,* which made its national film debut in 2012. She has published short stories and articles in numerous publications, including in the *Los Angeles Times, Poets & Writers* and many national literary journals. She is currently at work on her third novel. Schwartz lives with her family in Los Angeles.

For more information, go to www.leslieschwartz.com.

MY FIRST BOOK

Jerry Stahl

My first book was not my first book. I'd done six before it, generally publishing the first chapter as a short story in some glossy or literary mag or the other. The books were wild-ass — they were fun, they had lots of crazy writing. But they weren't particularly real (or, not to get too technical, *published*). Language — for me — was a way of hiding the truth, not revealing it. Not that I knew that then. I didn't know much, really. I was a feature magazine man. A grab'em by the neck in the first sentence and drag 'em around the house kind of guy.

No, I realized that I was, essentially, full of festive shit a bit later, when I actually was writing my actual first book. Along the way, there was the little matter of a year or ten spent strung out on heroin, destroying what life and/or career, relationship, family, health, future I might have had. Not to brag. Who knew addiction could be such a great career move?

But we only have a thousand words here, give or take, so let me cut to the proverbial chase. At the ripe age of thirty-nine, I found myself completely washed up, no prospects, living in the no-power basement of a crackhouse in Hollywood, with no functioning plumbing. The good people at L.A.

Noire landmark Musso & Franks, the oldest restaurant in
Hollywood, were uniformly thrilled to see me every morning
at eleven on the dot to use their toilet and order an orange
juice. Small. Just, you know, to maintain my dignity. And
this, by the way, was after I'd gotten clean.

In the midst of this high life, I bumped into Nancy
Gottesman, an editor for *Los Angeles Magazine*, where I used to
work sometimes, when I could still walk into a room without
making it smell. (Quick note, I never had the chance to thank
Ms. Gottesman, to whom I have not spoken in twenty years.
But without whose suggestion and support you would not be
reading this, and I would not be here. So, Nancy, wherever
you are, thanks!) We were standing right there on the Walk
of Fame, between Milton Berle and Mary Pickford. My old
friend and editor looked at me — and I knew the look: eyes
somewhere between sad and appalled. *Sappalled.* I felt —
well, you can imagine how I felt. Let's just say I was working
my way up to mortified. Mind you, as I say, I was off dope
now. Had been for a while. But I wasn't exactly styling. My
pants were clean — well, let's be honest, I only had one pair,
but when I wore them inside out, they were clean-adjacent. If
a little fetid. Just like the rest of me.

To make a long, shame-based story short, I told her what
I'd been up (or down) to, complete with big-boy gun-to-the-
head lameness in MacArthur Park, living *La Vida Cracka*.
(Did I mention, at one point, I had the bright idea of getting
off heroin by doing crack? A whole other story.) There were
other highlights: all the stations on the Junkie Cross — a
hospital spin-dry or two, post-rehab gig at McDonald's.

(You want rich literary turf, get yourself a job as Fry man, at Mickey D's, at the ripe age of thirty-eight. Sometimes, on lonely nights, I can still hear my nineteen-year-old co-workers, whispering to each other, *"I think he's retarded . . ."*) Onward to divorce, a relapse romance or two, re-entering the real world of living in somebody's garage and riding the bus with my little daughter, because Daddy didn't have a car. (And we're talking about Los Angeles, where not having a car packed slightly less prestige than leprosy.)

Anyway, my friend and former editor suggested I write about my experience. I say fine. Find myself — for the first time — writing about myself, as opposed to hiding behind the writing. Fast, as they say, forward, and I've got a magazine article in a long defunct shiny magazine called *Naked Brunch*. (Cute, but not my idea.) And not long after that, an agent gets in touch. We talk about a book. I have to do this thing called a "proposal." Imagine — a proposal to sum up your entire life. Putting that together, not to exaggerate, felt more difficult than actually living it. But never mind. Somehow I managed. Only to have the agent tell me it's just not right. His idea is a junkie version of *You'll Never Eat Lunch Again in This Town*, the epic Julia Phillips Hollywood tell-all. A fine book, no doubt, but absolute light-years from my own experience. I was, at best, a peripheral player in Hollywood. I'd had some experience, having slept my way to the middle by marrying a starting-out producer who needed a green card, who sort of kind of got me a couple TV gigs, after which I'd been fired from a variety of celebrated programs — most notably Twin Peaks, where I was canned (ah, Memories!) for turning in scripts with blood and hair on them. So, a dozen or so rejections later, I'm back where I started, maybe farther back, because I'd made the mistake of believing it was all going to happen.

It's a little blurry after that. What happens is, another agent gets in touch, she takes me on, we cook up a different proposal, and in no time at all, something like thirty publishing houses reject us. (In all honesty, I didn't know there were thirty publishing houses. In my narcissism and paranoia, I was convinced people were actually starting new publishing houses just so they could break my heart.) Finally, an editor friend of the agent's, a lovely if slightly manic woman whose primary accomplishment, I was given to understand, was a recently published tome entitled *The Bra Book*, decided to purchase my tome. At last!

The publisher was Warner Books, a corporate whale who was going to carry me off to a literary tomorrow. The advance was nice, too. I mean, by my standards. We're not talking the seven figure life-changers given to hotshot first time authors these days. Who am I kidding? We're not even talking six figures. No, I was still in the five-figure ghetto. But so what? To me, it was huge. When you've been wandering around babbling in Macarthur Park for a few years, and your last paying gig was sinking fry-baskets at McDonald's for minimum wage, the high fives look pretty good. At that point, Warner Books could have slipped me a fifty and a hot meal, and I'd have been grateful. Since getting clean, I'd lived free in that no-power crackhouse basement, in somebody's garage, above a porn store on Sunset Boulevard, and a few other deluxe addresses I've frankly forgotten.

But, back to those five figures: since I'd pretty much burned every friend I had (including a childhood pal who happened to be my lawyer), it wasn't like I could find anybody to read my contract, to comb through for the inevitable not-so-fine fine print. So that — thanks for asking — out of every dollar made on book sales, exactly one nickel went to paying back my advance. It was a position, I'd later learn, from which they were prepared to negotiate. But later was too late. Which may account for the fact that, despite becoming a best-seller, a movie, going into a couple of editions, etc., . . . I've yet to receive a penny's worth of royalties from my friends at Warner Books. Not to bitch — without them I'd probably be back at McDonald's, or more likely eating out of a dumpster behind it. So it's all gravy. Just, you know, *non-paying* gravy.

So there it is. A dream come true — which is, of course, where the hell really begins. Why, you ask? Well, for one thing, there's the matter of pressure. Massive, heart-in-mouth, 24-7 pressure. This wasn't about writing a book. This was about redemption at the high end and survival at the low. I had nothing else going on. No marketable skills, no real ability to get any, and thanks to the massive blessing of missing AIDS but getting Hepatitis C, I had the daily energy level of a ninety-year-old on chemo. But what the hell?

The challenge was to lean as far over the abyss and write about it without falling in again. Which, as it happened, I did, and ended up going back on dope while writing the book about my struggles to get off it. See, for me, writing was like walking a high wire over the Grand Canyon, and what drugs did was help you forget there was no net. I got about halfway before I fell. I clawed my way back out in time to be clean on *Oprah* — it was a theme show, "When Smart People Do Dumb Things."

Along with the fact that my terror over this book was about the prose — or not just — but about trying not to die, there were some niggling technical difficulties. The primary being that I was probably the last man in America to still write on a typewriter — an IBM Selectric to be exact, stolen from the back of a L.A. Department of Education truck by a homeboy I used to know who specialized in office products. But never mind. Nobody wanted to read from actual paper, so somehow — I can't even remember — I finagled some kind of Apple knock-off Australian computer. The company was named JoJo, or Hey Mate, or something ridiculous. I'm sure they're long out of business. And I remember the thrill when it stopped working entirely, and I marched it to some sleazoid computer repair shop, where, after a few minutes' cursory inspection, I was sent packing by the stylish young man in charge with the friendly suggestion, "Why don't you get a real fucking computer?"

But somehow I muddled through, turning in a chunky manuscript of 600-odd pages. (And I do mean odd.) A number that prompted major alarm from my editor before she even read them. I can still hear her shriek in the pay phone receiver. (No, I did not have a telephone either.) "For God's sake, we asked for two to three hundred pages, you've sent us over *a thousand!*"

Boy was *my* face red! What happened, see, was that in

my woeful ignorance of computer niceties, I had gotten the line setting wrong, so what I thought was double-spaced was actually one-and-a-half space. Thus, my already overblown near 700 pages of text swelled into nearly 1100. The result, needless to say, was that massive chunks of the book had to be cut. And what started out as a book mostly about being down and out and on heroin in Los Angeles somehow morphed — by virtue of these excisions — to a book about being in show business on heroin in Los Angeles, and my five minutes of television writing became the focal point of the memoir. The result being that, ever since, I have been pegged with the sobriquet "TV writer" by critics and assorted other literary aesthetes in a position to judge the work. To the point where, when the time comes, I have made plans for my tombstone to read, *"He only wrote three ALFS."*

But never mind. We all have our little cross to bear. For now, if I may be so bold — or pretentious — as to quote myself, let me end with the last line of the prologue that opened Permanent Midnight. *"I'm not sure the way this journey will go or where it's going. I only know I have to make the descent — to re-crawl into the inferno and pray to God in His Junkie Heaven I crawl back out again."*

Some days I'm still crawling. But who isn't? Thanks to that first book, and the world it opened before me, at least I made it to the other side.

Jerry Stahl is the author of seven books, including *Permanent Midnight, Bad Sex on Speed,* and *I, Fatty.* His work has also appeared in *Details, The New York Times, Esquire* and *The Believer,* among other places. Stahl has also written extensively for film and television, including, most recently, the HBO film *Hemingway & Gellhorn.*

ON TORCH

CHERYL STRAYED

My mom died when I was twenty-two and she was forty-five. She died of cancer, but it wasn't the way I thought a death by cancer would be — long and drawn out and cinematic. Instead, my mother was dead seven weeks to the day after her diagnosis. Her death was simple and ugly and it didn't feel even remotely like a movie. It felt like I had died with her, and in some ways, I did. The vision I'd previously had of my life died. I never had a relationship with my biological father, and though I had a stepfather, he couldn't continue being a stepfather to me in the face of his own loss. And so, I wandered forth, suddenly an orphan.

It was during this time that I was becoming a writer. I took a few writing workshops as an undergraduate. After meeting the writers who were my teachers, I knew that I wanted to be like them someday, writing and publishing books. By the time I was twenty-three and out of college, that's what I told people I was doing: writing a novel. It was literary realism; fictional, but informed by autobiography — a tale of a working class family and the rural northern Minnesota community that they lived in, about a mother dying young of cancer and about her kids and husband in their deepest sorrow.

But, the fact is, I wasn't writing a book. Instead, I was working a number of different jobs in order to pay the bills, and then quitting those jobs so I could travel around the country in my little pickup truck I'd named Myrtle. I was drinking herbal tea by day and red wine by night, and trying to figure out whether I should stay married to this sweet man I had married too young. I was shopping for cute dresses and funky boots in thrift stores, and hiking long nature trails, and getting a divorce. I was having sex with ridiculous and interesting people, and reading incredibly good books.

I was also writing, learning the writer's craft, journaling like mad and composing passages that I thought were chapters of my book. I applied for grants and residencies at writers' colonies, and whenever I won one I would quit whatever job I had and write. I would write like a motherfucker in a fever, sometimes writing for twelve or fourteen hours at a stretch. When the residency ended or the grant money ran out, I would find another job and talk to people about this novel I was writing. People would ask when I would finish the book, and almost always I would say within the year. And then another year would go by.

I know this sounds crazy, but it's true: I thought that *Torch* would write itself. Or rather, that something magical would happen that would make it be written, a force that would take me into its grips and enable me to write a book without too much suffering. Sometime around my thirtieth birthday, I looked up from all the hiking and shopping and odd-jobs and drinking of various concoctions and realized that my novel had not been written, and that it would not be written, not magically, in any case.

I had to write it. I had to. I had to. I said I would and so I would. I am not the kind of person who says she will do something and then does not do it. What I needed was time, I realized, which meant money, which, because I am without a trust fund, wealthy spouse, or even parents who would let me use their credit card from time to time, meant graduate school. I applied to MFA programs that offer their students full rides, got a full ride, and off to graduate school I went. At graduate school, I was given health insurance and a check each month simply for being there. My job was to write.

At last I had no excuses! I could write that novel about the working class family and the rural northern Minnesota community that they lived in, about the mother dying young of cancer and about her kids and husband in their deepest sorrow. Only now I didn't want to write that book, because at graduate school I quickly realized how deeply uncool that book was. My graduate school peers were not writing books about such things. They were writing books about people who were actually Volkswagen Beatles or composed entirely of paper. Or, if they were writing about real people, they were writing about them while also avoiding use of the letter e.

So, for a number of months I sat there at my computer knowing how stupid and non-experimental and pathetic I was to want to write that one idiotic story, and yet it was the only story I wanted to write, so there was nothing I could do but do it.

I called it *Torch* because I thought of myself as a torch singer, the one who sings a tale about a love that has disappeared, but goes on. I also liked how the word has connotations of both light and darkness, destruction and creation. I wanted to write the best novel that has ever been written in the world, but I finally had to let go of that and simply write the best novel I could write. A novel, I acknowledged, that might end up being mediocre at best, that might never be published or read or loved. Embracing those facts — that I could only write the story I wanted to write and only to the best of my abilities — was extremely liberating and important. It was what allowed me to finally get to work and write my novel.

Graduate school gave me a serious running start, but I didn't finish Torch until a little more than a year after I graduated. I was on an island in Brazil, at a writer's colony. I was ten weeks pregnant with my first child and relentlessly, around-the-clock nauseated. It was sunny outside, the middle of the day, but I was in my room, the shutters closed against the heat. I finished the last sentence of the last paragraph of the last page of my five-hundred page novel, and then I laid down on the floor and stared at the ceiling for an hour, listening to a Lucinda Williams song I love called "Bus to Baton Rouge" playing over and over and over and over again, her lovely voice singing to me from the tiny, tinny, awful speaker on my laptop computer. It was one of the purest moments of my life.

Cheryl Strayed is the author of the international bestseller *Wild*, the bestselling advice-essay collection *Tiny Beautiful Things*, and the novel *Torch*. Her writing has appeared in *The Best American Essays*, the *New York Times Magazine*, *The Rumpus*, the *Washington Post Magazine*, *Vogue*, *The Missouri Review*, *Creative Nonfiction*, *The Sun* and elsewhere. She lives in Portland, Oregon.

For more information, go to www.cherylstrayed.com.

UNDER THE DESK

Diana Wagman

For a long time, I was an unhappy screenwriter. I went to school for film, studied the art of the screenplay, and worked hard. I wrote seven scripts, each in a genre everybody — or at least somebody — was sure to want. I had a murder mystery, a romantic comedy, a buddy film, a family drama, and a cop movie. I pored over the film industry trade publications and the local newspapers, reading reviews, checking out what was popular, what was marketable, what would sell, sell, sell.

I grew up writing and wanting to be a writer. When I was seven, I arranged a special spot I called my writing place, under my mother's desk (Why under? Why not use the desk? As if writing isn't difficult enough!) with a pillow and pads of paper and my favorite pencils and a dictionary. I burrowed into my writing place and wrote stories, a penguin lost on an iceberg, a cowboy without a horse, a witch with a princess for a friend. It was fun. I loved it and I looked forward to huddling with my imagination.

But I grew up and went to school and I wasn't a good student and anyway in the public schools I went to there was never a creative writing assignment. I kept writing, but secretly. I could no longer fit under the desk, so I wrote in my bed at night. And I still loved it, but I didn't show it to anyone. By that time, I knew it was drivel: typical teenage angst no one would want to read.

Then, in college, I thought about writing as a career and foolishly thought screenwriters made money. I could write for movies. It was a craft. I could work at it, read books about it, figure it out and write high-concept, moneymaking scripts. And on the side, I could keep writing my secret stories that were now, I believed, still drivel, but filled with twenty-something angst.

I got married. I had children. I stopped writing my nighttime drivel. I worked only on screenplays. We needed the money. I made none. I had no meetings and no one reading. I couldn't even get my agent on the phone. He wouldn't take my call so I could fire him.

Seven screenplays — each one carefully constructed to star the most popular actor of the moment and to tell the story everyone wanted to see. I couldn't understand why it wasn't working. Eventually, I despaired. I stopped reading the trades. Stopped going to the movies. I'd sit down at my desk — I wrote on top of the desk now — and stare at the screen. I was beginning to hate writing.

And then a friend, Janet Fitch, unpublished at the time, well before the amazing success of *White Oleander*, took me to her writers' group. The leader gave an assignment, one word that we were supposed to free write six lines about. It was very loosy-goosy: I went home with the word "blue," and immediately put it out of my mind. I didn't do that kind of writing. I was much more calculating than that. But a few days later, sitting at my desk and not writing, I typed the word "blue." A picture came to me, of a woman in a blue world, with a blue car and a blue couch, wearing blue jeans. And then I imagined this woman totally encased in a blue bag. I began to write.

I wrote in prose. This wasn't a movie; it was not marketable. No actress would want to spend the majority of the film unseen inside a blue bag. It was just a story, and it got to be a bigger story, a story I really wanted to explore.

I continued writing screenplays and rewriting the ones I had, trying to make them more sellable. That was my work. But I ran to the computer every extra chance I got to write this story. I didn't know what it would be, but I had to write it down. It was fun. I loved it. I dreamed about my character, Martha, at night. She whispered in my ear as I was driving carpool or doing laundry or packing lunches in the morning. No screenplay had ever taken hold of my mind, my thoughts, my heart, the way Martha did. I started turning down social invitations to stay home and write.

I still thought of myself as a screenwriter. I was still trying to sell something. Through a friend, I had a meeting with Meg Ryan's producer, it went well, and for a moment I was buoyed, my ship was, if not coming in, at least visible on the horizon. Then they never called. I had to face it. My screenwriting career, the one that existed only in my imagination, was over. I was sad and I mourned and I turned to the prose I was writing as solace.

It wasn't yet a book. It was a collection of events and moments and observations about Martha in the blue bag.

Martha driving home in her blue car. Martha sleeping in blue sheets. I think I would, I know I could have written those stories forever. But my mother died suddenly and when I got back to writing, Martha's mother became my mother. The story had depths that weren't there before. Martha had a past. This blue bag became the logical outcome of all that had happened to her, and the perfect origin for what was to come.

I was bereft when I finished the draft. I wanted to keep at it, but the story was done. I couldn't say anymore. It had our mom in it, so I sent it to my older sister. She's a big reader and I wanted her to tell me it if I had truly written a novel.

What she said was "I don't know." She liked it. She recognized Mom and our stepfather, and some scenes from the past. She thought it was interesting, and she's a college professor and a wonderful teacher so she wanted to help me. She offered to send it to an English professor friend and I said no. I hadn't written it for that. I wrote it for me, because I had to, because I loved doing it, and especially because Martha wouldn't let me stop.

I didn't give the book to anyone else. It was just there and I thought I'd do something with it one day. Months went by. Three to be exact. And on July 17th, the phone rang and I answered.

"Diana Wagman?" a deeply southern voice said. "My name is JoAnne Prichard from the University Press of Mississippi and I'd like to buy your book."

She was the friend of my sister's, the English professor, and also Editor in Chief. I remember staring at the calendar that hung over the phone, noticing a birthday party my daughter was invited to that weekend. And it was my snack day for my son's soccer team. I didn't speak, because finally JoAnne said, "Hello? Is this Diana?" I didn't even know my sister had sent it to her. Joanne had to reassure me she had actually read the book I had written, that she hadn't confused me with someone else.

She said, "I can feel your love in this story."

I know. I was lucky. It's an incredible story, but the most important thing about it is that I had gone back to writing those secret stories I loved. Not to sell, not to make money, but because the actual act of writing gave me joy. I wrote *Skin Deep* out of pure love and it was the first thing I sold. That the established, experienced editor of that press wanted this very rough, unprofessional novel is a testament to the old adage: write from your heart.

The coda to the story is that JoAnne and I worked on that book for months, sometimes page by page. I learned a lifetime's worth of writing knowledge from her. The book came out and was very favorably reviewed in *The New York Times Sunday Book Review*. The next day, the phone rang and it was a producer wanting to option my book. And he wanted me to write the screenplay. The first real money I ever made from screenwriting, was because of this book.

Shortly thereafter, my agent called. "Saw you in the *Times*," he said. And I fired him.

Diana Wagman is the author of four novels. Her second, *Spontaneous*, won the 2001 PEN West Award for Fiction. Her latest, *The Care & Feeding of Exotic Pets,* was chosen as a Barnes & Noble Discover Pick. Her screenplay, *Delivering Milo,* was produced starring Albert Finney and Bridget Fonda. She has had short stories and essays published, most recently in *Conjunctions* and *The Colorado Review,* and is an occasional contributor to the *Los Angeles Times.*

For more information, go to www.dianawagman.com.

WANNA PUBLISH A BOOK? EASY: SELL YOUR SOUL

ERIC MILES WILLIAMSON

I'd been writing short stories about my youth, my upbringing, for a decade, but after my first divorce, I decided to write a novel. I had nothing but time, since I didn't have anyone to abuse and be shitty to anymore. I then taught at Houston Community College. We imitation professors didn't have to hold office hours (we didn't have offices) and we rarely had meetings. Meet with the young inner-city scholars, give them A's and B's, tell them to transfer to Harvard, collect my paycheck and go to the liquor store. I didn't need to write a novel, since I had a job and it had no research requirements. I just thought it might be a good idea if an English professor teaching novels to his students actually knew what the fuck he was talking about since he'd tried to write one himself — unlike professors who teach poetry and have never written a poem, who teach short stories and have never published one, who teach Shakespeare and have never acted, done makeup, worked the lights, or hammered together and painted a stage.

Besides, I figured the world needed to hear about

construction workers. Only Pietro di Donato (who wrote the book in the Depression era and whose father was an Italian bricklayer) had addressed the subject, as far as I could tell then, by writing a book called *Christ in Concrete*. I'd been a union construction worker, a guniter, as a young man, shooting concrete from a high-pressure hose, and I wanted to tell the story. Partially because I wanted people to respect and admire me for coming from the lower class and escaping it, partially because my blue collar father thought I was a pussy because I had college degrees and I wanted to become a success to prove he was an asshole and shame him, partially because I wanted to be a better professor, and partially because I thought I was the greatest writer America had ever produced, even though I'd written next to nothing and didn't know my ass from a hole in the ground.

I finished the novel in 1991, when I was thirty years old — about the same age Melville finished *Moby Dick* — and I was certain that I was as good as Melville and suspected that my novel, *Two-Up* was better, and by far. I titled it *Two-Up* after a hand signal that men on the job site used as a universal metaphor for all that is good and right and macho.

When I'd printed out the last page, I got drunk and went to the seedy district in Houston everyone refers to as Westheimer, so called after its main thoroughfare. The street back then was lined with gay clubs, lesbian clubs, hoboes, tattoo parlors, prostitutes and pimps, bookstores, drug dealers, bars, junkies, ethnic restaurants, and halfway houses. It was a splendid place, neon nights and dazed afternoons, the smell of humid body odor and flowers, of garbage and desperation. I walked into a tattoo parlor and got myself a tattoo on my chest of a scorpion, a reminder to myself that like the scorpion, I had the capability of killing myself. And writing that first book, *Two-Up*, nearly killed me. I came close to losing my job because I'd cancel classes when I was on a writing and drinking binge, I lost my sense of self, sometimes waking from dreams convinced the characters were going to kill me for writing about them, and, according to my friends, I lost my mind, babbling incoherently when I talked, staggering the petrochemical streets of Houston in the odd hours and drinking malt liquor with anyone who'd listen to me in alleys, on park benches, and beneath bridges.

I'd worked on the novel for three and a half years, wrote 600 pages of first-draft, self-indulgent slop the first year and a half, then spent two years trimming the book down to less than 300 pages. I thought I'd written a masterpiece. I bought Robert Phillips, then Director of the prestigious Creative Writing Program at the University of Houston and author of some thirty books, a 1.75 of Dewars and went to his house unannounced. I foisted upon him the manuscript and asked him to help me get an agent, and he did. He cracked the bottle and we drank one together. The agent, Jake Elwell, a young guy from a powerful New York agency, sent *Two-Up* to sixty different publishing houses, and they all said no thanks. I was still America's greatest author, it's just that every editor in America was an idiot, is what I told myself. I didn't lose confidence. I just got pissed off and blamed everything from my humble background, to the conspiracy of Ivy League writers like Roth and Oates and Updike taking up too much space on the presses, to the presses not being able to publish unknowns because they had too much other work to do.

Two-Up, the first draft of which I completed in 1991, didn't get published until 2006, fifteen years after I "finished" it. When it got accepted for publication, I spent another year revising it and made 20,000 edits, according to my computer, ignoring my newborn son and my beautiful wife, who could have used some help taking care of the home, staying up until four in the morning, passing out drunk with open gas-flames blasting into the Missouri night and endangering all of us after yet another twelve-hour day of editing.

Writing *Two-Up* made me an addict. And don't kid yourself: writing, creating art, when you're not getting paid for it, is an addiction. Why the fuck would someone sacrifice their personal relations, their job, their family, their friends, their sanity, their soul, their health and maybe their life with little hope of gain of any kind if they weren't a hopeless addict? Art, generally, and attempting to write literature, specifically, is a fix, a hot shot into euphoria and misery, no different than what compels comedians — who are also artists — into the throes of ecstasy and suicide. Artists are maniacs, and I've behaved like one every time I've written a book. So I stop writing and try to be normal, try to pay attention to my wife and children, mow the lawn, eat, for fuck sakes. And then my fire is gone, I'm a schmuck with a lawnmower and a clean carpet and dishes in the cabinets instead of strewn about the apartment or house, hair neat and combed and checkbook balanced, and I get depressed and just sit around all day drinking beer and pacing. Then I get back to writing a book, and I become a psychotic, and everything's good again, except it's not. It's the same pattern as drug addicts or alcoholics, both of which writers tend to be, especially when they're not writing, the chemical addiction substituting for the writing addiction.

Two-Up had been rejected by just about every publisher in the nation, so I scrapped it and got back to work on the short stories I'd been writing since I was 19 years old. I wanted the published book. I needed the fix. I wanted the love.

That book, which ended my first published one, is *East Bay Grease,* originally published by Picador USA and translated into many languages. It's recently been re-released by Writers Tribe Books on its Modern Classics series. *East Bay Grease* took me nineteen years to write. I started it, I suppose, when I was nineteen years old, when I wrote an early draft of the short story that was eventually to become the first chapter. All but one of the fourteen chapters were published, first in periodicals such as *The Georgia Review, The Virginia Quarterly Review, The Iowa Review,* and so forth, major journals, as short stories. I had no idea I was writing a novel as I wrote those stories. But when they reached critical mass, I realized I had a book about my youth, my bildungsroman, my coming-of-age book. It got accepted for publication in 1998 and was published when I was thirty-eight, in 1999.

East Bay Grease was my training ground. I read three books a day for nearly twenty years while I was writing it, and nearly every sentence in *East Bay Grease* is a modulation of or riff on the work of a great dead writer: Conrad, Melville, Henry Miller, Celine, Shakespeare, Joyce, Proust, Flaubert, Poe, Hemingway, Faulkner, McCarthy, Baldwin, Dickens, Dostoevsky, Milton, Barry Hannah, Barthelme (not the Master's idiot little brothers — what are their names anyway? — but Donald, the Great One), Sukenick, Twain, did I say Melville? I wanted to write stories that my college professors and my dad, who pumped gas, would all enjoy, but for different reasons.

I knew I was a writer, and serious, when I gave up my job as a college professor, sold all my possessions, including my LP collection and my stereo, sold my car and cashed out my retirement, to move to New York City. I didn't care if I went there and starved: I wanted the world to know that I was the greatest writer alive. I wanted the Nobel Prize, and not just once, but year after year because there wasn't another motherfucker who dared have the audacity to accept it while I was alive, is what. I wanted my father to see his pussy-ass son with a million bucks in his checking account. Bite me, Pop. Pump some gas. Maybe I'll loan you a ten-spot when you need a case of Busch or Schlitz. On the other side of town I'll be drinking Jim Beam or Smirnoff, the fancy uptown hooch.

As I'm writing this, I'm thinking: What the fuck? Did I actually write a good first novel — twice? I reckon I did. I go to international book festivals about four times a year (they like me in France), and when I get off the plane, my Mercedes limo takes me to my fancy hotel where I do photo-shoots and interviews on national television and radio. I gots me two first novels what I talks about, amigo. Mights be a perfesser now, but I can't get the stink of my lower-class upbringing out of my skin or off my tongue. Over there, in Europe, they love this: I'm like Bukowski (they call me "The Erudite Bukowski" and "The Last Beat") or Hunter S. Thompson, a clown-like madman, probably just because I use the words shit and fuck and asshole and cunt. Doesn't the fuck every motherfucking fuck say the fucking word fuck? What the fuck?

Got *East Bay Grease* published in the usual way. Because I was in the right place at the right time, living in New York city and drinking booze with the right rich fucks, the fucks.

You know, in NYC, actors and actresses carry their headshots in their pockets, pretty pictures of themselves without pimples leaking yellow and green cottage cheese pus and without sweat and mucus oozing down their faces. Those pictures rock. The real life people in our advertisements are disgusting, anorexic junkie basket-cases.

When I lived in New York, I was no better than the wannabe actors and actresses. I went to all the parties, I went to the famous "writer" bars like The Cedar in the Village, hung around the right bookstores, kissed ass at readings performed by the famous people, finagled invites to the awards ceremonies (NBCC, National Book Awards, American Academy of Arts and Letters). I weaseled my way into an editorship of Chelsea, one of the oldest and most respected literary journals in the country at the time.

I convinced the editors of Chelsea to let me start a book review section. I did this with mal-intent, for self-serving reasons, not to help the journal. See, if you assign a book for review, and run a favorable review of that book, the publisher of the book and the author are both very happy people. Now this: make sure that the books you review are published by houses you want to be on, and also be sure to review books by people who edit literary journals. Do them a favor, they do you a favor. I got published in *The Southern Review*, one of the most stately journals in the nation, because I published their editor. I published him, he published me. Then I reviewed his book favorably in *The Houston Chronicle*. Prostitutes are much more honest plying their trades than are writers who are scrambling for publication, and then recognition, and then love, and then immortality.

I got an NEA grant when I was living in New York City. I got the grant because my friend at the time, Dagoberto Gilb, was on the committee and recognized my work in the pile. He sent me a postcard after I got the award and told me it was his doing, surely thinking that I'd later return a favor, now that I had more power than I already did, which favor, of course, I produced, many times.

What did I do with that NEA grant, $20,000 bucks? Well, because of Bush senior, the grant was now taxable, and so that meant I had to set aside six grand of it for taxes, even though it was taxes that paid for the grant, fucked up America. I paid down my credit cards two grand. And then I spent $12,000 throwing a party in my honor in New York in my nine-room apartment in Manhattan. I bought fancy mirrors, fancy furniture, and fancy clothes for my then-wife (#2) and myself, white clothes to contrast what everyone wears in New York, since to own a white suit, as Mark Twain says, you got to own seven. I bought $8K of booze, keggars and expensive hooch. I had a caterer. Fancy cheese and meat, fruit and veggie platters, $150 a bottle champagne. Nearly 200 people attended my party.

They didn't come for the free hooch and food, because in Manhattan that shit's everywhere, at every party and reading and reception. They came because they were scared. What I did to get that crowd of assholes in power (because these were the major writers and editors and agents of New York — hell, people came from something like twenty states to attend my party) was this: I called a famous writer.

I told that writer, an ass-sucking Ivy-Leaguer, that another famous ass-sucking Ivy-Leaguer was attending, and ass-sucker #1 should attend because ass-sucker #2 would be there. And so she said she'd come. Then I called ass-sucker #3 and told him that ass-suckers #1 and #2 would be attending, and so he shouldn't miss out or else fellow ass-suckers would note his absence. Then I called suck-ass x and y and z and all through the alphabet and that's how it went. I had all the big players there in my apartment on West 46th Street and 9th Avenue jockeying to explain their relationship to me, the great writer who threw the party — which lasted three days, people fucking in my bathroom and on the roof of my five-story walk-up — the great new arrival in Manhattan.

During the party, my then-wife and I agreed that we'd pretend we didn't know each other and that we'd promote each other's work. I told people she was a great poet, and she told people I was a great fiction writer, and we never even looked each other in the eye, for days. To a famous writer or editor she'd say, in a conspiratorial whisper, "Somebody told me that Eric Miles Williamson is here. Have you met him? Where is he? I'd like to meet him. Do you think he's married? Does he have a girlfriend or a lover? It's his party, you know. There are rumors about him. I hear he is not only a great writer, but he has an oil fortune. He's from Texas!" And I'd sling the same shtick about her.

Pretty promptly, all the stories I was writing were getting published in major venues. I went to parties at George Plimpton's house, with the good folks from Harpers and Esquire and Playboy. I was famous, in Manhattan at least. Only cost me $12K, my retirement from the community college in Texas, and my soul.

A few weeks later I attended a publication party in SoHo at a mafia bar owned by a Princeton Italian who'd started himself a literary journal and published me. At the party was Gordon Lish and lots of other power players in the NY scene. I sat drinking next to a morose and somber man, expensive Scotch, $200 bucks a bottle stuff. After a while, the bartender just gave us the bottle and we poured our own drinks.

"Why you here?" I asked.

"One of my authors is published in the journal."

"You support your authors like this?"

"Why not," he said. He lifted his tumbler. "Free booze."

We drank.

At four in the morning, I reached into my sport coat pocket (a fashionably black Goodwill jacket) and pulled out my manuscript — carried it around with me like actors and actresses carry around their glossy head-shots — and asked him to read it. Both our heads were bowed low, and we'd started on our second bottle of Scotch.

When he kind of finished it — I don't think his eyes could focus enough to actually read the story — I asked him if he could sell a novel that was as good as that story. He said he could. He gave me his card. He was an agent at Curtis Brown, Ltd., the oldest agency in the western hemisphere. They represented Henry James. They represented D.H. Lawrence. They represented Adolph Hitler.

The next day — four hours later, sweating beads of hangover booze-curd from my forehead — I showed up at the office at 10 Astor Place in the Village and gave him my manuscript.

Two weeks later, I had a book contract for *East Bay Grease* from Picador USA.

Instant success. It only took about twenty years of sucking ass and scheming. Try it sometime. It feels great, and your children and ancestors will be proud.

First novel? I don't know how you did it, but that's how I did it. It was the most ugly enterprise of my life, and the residue of it coats me with filth.

In 2009, **Eric Miles Williamson** was named by France's *Transfuge* magazine one of the "douze grands écrivains du monde" — one of the twelve great authors of the world. His first novel, *East Bay Grease,* was a PEN/Hemingway finalist and listed by the *Los Angeles Times Book Review* as one of the "Best Books of 1999," and its sequel, *Welcome to Oakland,* was named the second-best novel of 2009 and one of the top forty novels of the decade by *The Huffington Post.* His novel, *Two-Up* was named one of the top 100 books of the 2006 by both *The Kansas City Star* and *The San Jose Mercury News*. *The Atlantic Monthly* said his first book of criticism, *Oakland, Jack London, and Me* was "One of the least politically correct texts of our time, and *Kirkus* said his second book of criticism, *Say It Hot: Essays on American Writers Living, Dying, and Dead* is "unhinged."

WRITE UNTIL IT'S OVER

Alan Watt

In April '98 I flew from Los Angeles to Toronto to perform standup comedy at six clubs over a six-week period. In that time I wrote the first draft of my first novel, *Diamond Dogs*.

I began my comedy career in Toronto and had been going up there regularly to work, but this time I wasn't looking forward to seeing any of the old crowd. Over the past couple of years, things had gotten bad. The core group of eighty comics used to meet at The Pilot, a low rent bar near the club where comics converged after their gigs, where we drank and told lies to each other until closing. But something happened in the last couple of years. Four comics took their lives. Stand up draws desperate souls, and these recent events made it difficult to pretend that we were just young rowdy jokesters charting our course to stardom.

In fact, most of us were no longer in our twenties, and it was becoming clear that making a crowd of drunken yuppies do spit takes did not mean you had mastered the form. It takes a while to realize you're a hack, and for some of us, the awareness made us scuttle in retreat like cockroaches at dawn.

Comics — without exception — are all looking for their fathers. They drink, take drugs, and attempt to bed women (though comics have little game) in pursuit of dad's approval. They also kill themselves at a rate much higher than the national average.

Years earlier, I told my old man a story that I planned to write. The idea came to me on my midnight drives from the club in Toronto back to my folk's farm, an hour away. I would turn the headlights off and play chicken with myself, driving through inky blackness on deserted country roads, counting to three, four, five, until my adrenaline spiked, and I would turn the lights back on, out of breath, high, thrilled to be alive. I was flooded with adrenaline from the show and as I came down, this was how I tried to recapture the love.

On these drives the story came to me. A kid kills another kid on the highway. He panics — puts the body in the trunk — and goes home. His father is the Sherriff of this small town. The father discovers the body. He disposes of it, and it is never spoken about. It would be a story of family secrets, where the kid would begin to understand, over the course of a few days, the truth of his mother's disappearance a decade earlier.

Each night, I drove this stretch of road, and a new piece of the story revealed itself. I kept asking "What if" and the screw kept tightening.

One day, I sat in my father's dining room and told him this yarn I'd been spinning. The story twisted and turned. There were surprises and reversals, and when I was done, he was silent.

"What do you think," I asked.

He cleared his throat. "Is that all you can write about is goddamn fathers and sons?"

I was devastated. But it was true. My stand up act was replete with jokes about our relationship. Sometimes it felt less like comedy, and more just a cry for help.

When I was little a kid came up to me. He said, "My dad can beat up your dad." I said: "Really? How much would that cost me?"

The years passed. I moved to L.A. to do standup. I got signed by a big-shot talent agency and wrote screenplays that didn't sell. I wrote what I thought would make me famous. But this story kept nagging, and one day, I couldn't take it anymore. I had a revelation: *I have been writing every single day for thirteen years. I have sold nothing.* I did the math and concluded that, at best, I was a mediocre writer, and yet . . . this was all I'd ever wanted to do. Therefore, I decided to put all my chips on red. *From now on, I will write for myself.*

I wrote the first draft of *Diamond Dogs* in hotel rooms over the course of six weeks. I began each morning with a prayer. I lay in bed and told God to write the pages for me. Tell me what to write, and I will. And I did. I wrote in a fever, some days expelling five thousand words onto the page.

I wrote for eight and ten hours straight, sometimes literally right up until the MC was introducing me onstage. It was like this story was happening in real time, and I was taking dictation. The story had lived in my subconscious for so long that it blasted out of me. The first-person voice surprised me. The kid was funny and sort of guileless, consumed with self-loathing and too young to hide it. His thoughts poured onto the page amidst this plot that galloped along.

When I got to the climax, the scene where the boy confronts his father, I was stuck. Paralyzed. It was as if, from out of nowhere, I was being asked to fight this battle for the universe, and was handed a garden trowel.

I cursed God in my hotel room. How could you take me this far, only to dump me at the finish line. How dare you? I did everything you asked. I served you obediently, and you tricked me. Is this a joke? Fuck you.

I cursed Him in my journal until my pen tore through the paper. My words got huge. A sentence filled the page. I wasn't writing from my wrist, I was taking swings at the page. How dare you abandon me! I leapt to my feet and marched to my hotel room door. "Get out," I told God. I slammed the door. I shouted at Him in the hallway, "I'll write it myself!"

And I did.

I banged out eight pages in an hour. The kid went toe to toe with dad. It was brutal. Horrendous. I wrote through my tears. And when it was over, I stared at the page, shocked at what had happened. The ending wouldn't let me indict the old bastard. No, it was more complicated than that. The man loved his son. He would do anything for him. This love lay underneath a mountain of scar tissue and years of secrets and lies. There was some kind of order to the universe that I refused to believe until that moment.

I sat on the couch in my room and listened to my breath. I looked up. I don't know what I was looking at, but I said out loud, "You didn't leave did you?"

And this voice that had been guiding me through the

process said to me, clear as a bell: "No." It said to me. "That was your father."

Everything I wanted came to me in that moment. I understood something that I could not have understood any other way. I told the story. I told the truth. No, that's not correct. The truth told me. And for some reason, call it grace, call it mercy, I wrote it down.

I wrote until it was over. Not done. Over.

It was a Saturday afternoon. The sky was pale. I stood at the window of my hotel room and for an hour I stared down at the afternoon traffic. That Monday I flew back to L.A. with four yellow legal pads full of words.

I transcribed it onto my computer and gave it to a friend to read. She liked it, and through another friend I got it to a book agent in New York, and a week later my agent auctioned it for a lot of money.

I know. I'm lucky.

For thirteen years I wrote. Every day. Every single day. On the subway, at home, in cars and in coffee shops, drunk and sober, when she left me, when I left her: for thirteen years I wrote. I wrote in my dreams. I woke up muttering incoherent words and watching them appear on a page somewhere in the back of my brain stem. For thirteen years I wrote down words. I wrote until I no longer cared if anyone ever read a word that I wrote. I wrote until I felt nothing but sheer gratitude for the experience of having written. I just kept writing until I stopped asking why. And then I wrote this book.

Alan Watt has won a number of awards for his writing including France's Prix Printemps (best foreign novel) for his first novel, *Diamond Dogs*. He is the author of numerous books on writing, including *The 90-Day Novel*, *The 90-Day Rewrite*, and *The 90-Day Screenplay*. He founded L.A. Writers' Lab in 2002 as a place for writers to deepen their craft by learning the process of marrying the wildness of their imaginations to the rigor of story structure.

For more information, go to www.lawriterslab.com.

MY FIRST BOOK(S)

David L. Ulin

"There's nothing to writing.
All you do is sit down at a typewriter and open a vein."

— Red Smith

– *I* –

I wrote my first first book over the course of three months, from July 23rd to October 23rd, 1979. Four weeks in, I turned eighteen. This was a novel, and not the first I'd attempted; in fifth grade, I had written forty pages of a saga called *Gangwar in Chicago*, inspired by *The Godfather* and taking place in a city where I'd never been. Setting the story in Chicago meant scouring the map in World Book for locations: Canal Street, I recall, was one. I chose it because I knew Canal Street in New York, and it seemed the sort of landscape in which a gang war could take place. To this day, I have never seen Chicago's Canal Street, despite the twenty years I spent visiting my wife's family in a suburb on the North Shore.

The other novel, the one I finished, was motivated almost

entirely by a specific case of envy — of my friend Fred, who
had spent the same summer working on a novel of his own.
Fred and I were high school writing buddies, confiding to
each other, as we wandered the grounds of our New England
boarding school, that we both wanted to win the Nobel Prize.
Now, he'd written a campus novel, tracing his difficulties as a
one-year senior, parsing the school's social hierarchy in a way
that seemed enlightening and true. Fred was more serious,
more focused; he not only knew what symbolism was, but
also how to use it. It made sense that he would write a novel,
and that it would be good. A year later, he would write
another one . . . and then we lost track of each other, until six
or seven years later, when his short stories started to appear
in magazines.

For me, Fred's novel represented something of a
provocation — not on his part, but on mine. I was jealous
of his talent, of his motivation; I was jealous that he had the
discipline to write. I'd wanted to be a writer since the age of
seven, but my body of work, such as it was, consisted largely
of misfires: stories, plays, novel fragments, essays, almost all of
them undone. My problem was follow-through; I'd begin with
great excitement, only to grow bored. Even when I finished
something, I couldn't say how I had done it, and my writing
was full of political and social pieties, soapbox sentiments that,
even to me, rang false. I liked (and why not?) the idea of being
a writer better than I liked writing, which to this day remains
an unsteady process, a balancing act between expectation and
an almost willful lack of expectation, between my aspiration
and my failure, between what I want and what I cannot do.

I'm familiar with this now, this ongoing frustration, but then, it used to drive me crazy, the imperfection that sets in with the first written word.

I began my first first book the same way I'd begun nearly every piece of writing I had, until then, yet attempted: longhand, in a spiral notebook. Inside the front cover, I inscribed, as epigraph, a lyric from Lynyrd Skynyrd: "I've seen a lot of people who thought they were cool / But then again, Lord, I've seen a lot of fools." Skynyrd wasn't my favorite band, but the lines felt redolent, reflective of an idea, a message I wanted to express. This was a trick, of course, a way to push myself; then, as now, I was a sucker for a good quote, keeping notebooks full of them, taken from books and movies and records and other corners of the culture, as if together these artifacts might add up to a collage of who I wished to be. I wrote an opening scene, about returning to school for my senior year after eight weeks at Harvard Summer School, sitting in a dorm on the Yard, smoking dope from the moment I woke up in the morning until the moment my eyes drooped closed at night. That would be the story of my senior year also, or at least part of the story of my senior year, albeit the part I was least equipped to tell. I was enamored, then, of drug literature — *The Doors of Perception*, *The Teachings of Don Juan*, *Fear and Loathing in Las Vegas*, *The Electric Kool-Aid Acid Test* — seeing such books as reports from the frontlines of consciousness, a territory I meant to inhabit as well. I wanted to do something similar with my own book, to articulate my self-indulgence, my (*say it*) self-destruction, as self-exploration, although it's difficult, I would learn, to frame getting stoned as a reason to be. This is the first lesson: Don't write to serve an agenda, but rather to serve a story, the novel as instrument of narrative, steeped in character, conflict, interiority. I worked sporadically for a month or so, presenting myself as epic antihero; like Jack Kerouac, I aspired to make myth of autobiography. Yet unlike Kerouac, who wrote *The Subterraneans* in three days and *Big Sur* in ten, I wasn't producing — just bits and pieces here and there. By late August, I had composed maybe fifteen pages, barely a beginning. Fred's novel loomed in the imagination. I needed a different strategy.

I don't remember where I got the idea to use a tape recorder, only that once I did, it felt as though I'd found a key. Starting in September, I embarked on a new routine, staying up all night, fortifying myself with bong hits, talking, talking, talking in a series of eight hour jags, midnight to 8:00 a.m., evening after evening until the story had been told. I was in the first few months of a year off — a decision reached, at first, by choice, then rendered necessary by the crash-and-burn of my senior year, a crash-and-burn I meant to evoke in the novel, even as I sought to recover from it (reapplying to college, trying to build a new relationship with my parents) in my life outside the book. I lived, that fall, in my childhood room, redecorated as disaffected teenage lair: stereo, shelves full of paperbacks, batik tapestries hanging from the ceiling, low light in the corners, closed and cloistered, a safe space in which to incubate a world. Thinking about it, I see a link between the book I was dictating (*how I got here*) and the narrative I was trying to create for college (*how I will move on from here*), two sides of a legend about reinvention, in which my mistakes could only make me stronger, inoculating me against myself. And yet, I understand now, both were fantasies, bits of bravado, stories I wanted to believe so badly I convinced myself that they were true.

Such was the case also with my first first book, which was never a novel in any real sense of the word. Once I stopped talking, my father paid to have my tapes transcribed, and I was left with 434 typed pages of testimony loosely dressed as fiction, devoid, for the most part, of punctuation, paragraphs, proper spellings . . . any of the hallmarks of polished prose. My intent had been to circumvent my laziness, or fear, or lack of commitment — my inability to see a project through from start to finish — by short-shrifting the process, by dictating a draft so I could jump straight into revision, where, I liked to tell myself (correctly, as it turned out), the real writing would be done. But what did I know of real writing? Only that it was too hard. As for the manuscript, I sat down with it a time or two, but it was impenetrable. Blocks of text, phonetic misspellings, not to mention all those endless sentences, digressions, and other conversational misdirections. The trouble with dictation, I had no choice but to acknowledge, was that talking wasn't writing, that the former was discursive while the latter was, had to be, more controlled. The key to writing, in other words, was *writing*, which was the second lesson, and it was one that I'd remember when I began my second first book.

– II –

I wrote my second first book over the course of twenty months, from June 18th, 1982 to February 26th, 1984. This was a novel also, the first I'd attempted since my experiment with spoken prose. I wrote in longhand in a succession of spiral notebooks, inspired by an epigraph from Goethe: "Know thyself? If I knew myself, I'd run away." Later, during revisions, I appended a second epigraph, borrowed from the Sex Pistols: "I don't believe illusion because too much is for real."

Here, too, I was motivated (initially, at least) by jealousy. I started the book during the summer between my sophomore and junior years in college, which I spent in Cambridge, Massachusetts, working in a pizza joint soon to be named worst in greater Boston by *Boston Magazine*. My best friend, Steve, had transferred to NYU Film School, where he was making his first short movies, and in our almost daily phone conversations, I would listen as he laid out creative issues: script, shots, story, the challenges of collaborating with a loose crew of fellow students, all of whom were caught up in projects of their own. From two hundred miles away, it sounded like a slice of heaven, although film was not then (nor is it now) my thing. What stirred me, rather, was that Steve was doing *it*, whatever that meant, pursuing something that seemed like destiny. I was twenty that summer, turning twenty-one in August, and I felt a growing pressure to be (how do I put this without reservation or irony?) *great*. I still recall those three months in Cambridge through the filter of what I was reading: Camus, Walker Percy, Frederick Exley, and perhaps most important,

Henry Miller, whose stirring admonition in the early pages of *Tropic of Cancer* — "We have evolved a new cosmogony of literature. It is to be a new Bible — *The Last Book*. All those who have anything to say will say it here — *anonymously*. After us not another book — not for a generation, at least" — I took as a call to arms. That was what I wanted also: to produce my own *Last Book*, to get everything I'd ever thought or felt on paper, to connect with the core of not just literature but also being, and in so doing to write my way out of circumstance and into fate. I had begun writing long fiction again that year: an 11,000-word short story on which I worked mostly in the back of college classrooms, writing feverishly while my professors talked about whatever, under the illusion (if they were paying attention at all) that I was taking notes.

The novel started as a monologue, the novel started as a conceit. The idea was to do something short and striking, something like *The Stranger*, one hundred fifty pages in and out. Like Meursault, my protagonist was alienated, a first-person narrator alone in a room. Early on, I decided that the novel should unfold in six chapters, since the classic structure of the epic involved twelve; what I was writing was half an epic, the story of a boy, not unlike myself but utterly adrift. Eventually, those six chapters grew to twelve, then to twenty-four: not half but twice an epic, in length if nothing else. This was in the late 1980s, after I blew up my 250-page draft into a 564-page revision, a manuscript so bloated that it literally could not be read. That's a part of this story, although maybe not the most important part of this story; I have not looked at that set of pages in a very long time.

But here's what is important: I sabotaged my own book. I did this in two ways, first by overthinking and then by overtalking, by telling everyone I knew everything about the work. Again, I was driven by theme, by concept. My first chapter was a thirty-page ode to masturbation, a metaphor (much too obvious) for the disconnection at the novel's heart. It took me that whole first summer to complete it, and when I was done, I had no idea where to go. I wrote a second chapter in third person, experimented with past and present tenses; two-thirds of the way through the first draft, I was so lost, so hopelessly unmoored, that I decided to start again. That second draft became the book, or a version of it: I wrote my way through in nine months, start to finish, turning it in as my senior thesis, the story of a boy who could not deal with death and, in trying to run from it, wreaked havoc on everyone he'd ever known.

What did I understand of this? Nothing, it turned out, although that was not the difficulty. All these years later, I've learned that writing is an art of the unknown, that we write what we don't know, rather than what we do. "I write," Joan Didion tells us, "entirely to find out what I'm thinking, what I'm looking at, what I see and what it means. What I want and what I fear." Implicit in such a statement is how little she grasps when she begins. What I didn't know — what I wouldn't know for decades — was how to sit with my uncertainty, how to let a narrative develop, how to let it be uncontrolled. I wanted to write not just a novel but a landmark novel, one that made big statements about what it meant to live in the world. Because of this, perhaps, the draft I finished felt thin to me: It was just the story of a boy, after all. I set it aside for two years, trying to figure out how to rework it; I talked and talked about its aesthetics, about what I wanted it to say. By the time I picked it up again, in late 1986, I felt straight-jacketed, defined by it: Every conversation, no matter how trivial, seemed to cycle back to the subject of the book. The pressure was enormous, overwhelming, as if I were being watched. I spent two years on a third draft, another twelve months on a fourth . . . and then the novel petered out, over-written, over-discussed, picked at like the desiccated corpse of something I had killed by giving it too much attention, or the wrong sort of attention, something I should have abandoned years before.

Or no, not abandoned — not necessarily. This is complicated, and it's a lesson I feel as if I'm just now learning, the great lesson, maybe, of this book. This past winter, nearly thirty years after I completed it, I read the novel in its shorter, senior thesis form. It's an apprentice work, no doubt about it, a boy writing about the difficulty of being a certain kind of boy. And yet, there's also something compelling, a sense I get of myself as a young writer struggling to find a voice. I keep getting in my own way, loading up the narrative with frills, stylistic and otherwise, but there are places where the writing starts to sing. I remember the finest moments of its creation: when, deep in the middle of the book, I would go for a walk, have a conversation, read something in the newspaper, and all of it, every last whisper, would have some necessary link to what I was trying to construct. "Once you're into a story," Eudora Welty once observed, "everything seems to apply:

what you overhear on a city bus is exactly what your character would say on the page you're writing. Wherever you go, you meet part of your story." I had not experienced this during my last attempt at novel-making because in that case I had not really been *writing*, although here I absolutely was. Reading my old manuscript, I was drawn back to those moments, that sense of connection, the idea of being so present in the book, *in the world*, that it felt as if all my boundaries had dissolved. This is what writing requires, and it's a message I have carried with me . . . this and one other, which is never to talk about what I'm working on. An obvious point, perhaps, and not unrelated to my first first book. But then, I'm a slow learner, especially when it comes to recognizing that there is talking and there is writing, and for me, no way for them to co-exist.

– III –

I wrote my third first book over the course of five years, from January 9th, 1998 to January 3rd, 2003. It was a work of nonfiction that began with an elaborate lie, and even here, in telling you about it, I am lying also, for this was not my first book but my fourth. By the time I finished writing it, I had published three other books: a chapbook of poetry and two edited anthologies. It's a lie, also, that I began the book in 1998, since it grew out of a long article I had written for *LA Weekly*, published in April 1999; it was this I started the year before.

Why all this emphasis on lying? At the risk of confusing matters, I didn't — still don't — see it that way. The lie that opened the book was not a willful falsehood but a misperception, a conflation of memory, a way of getting at what let's call (yes) emotional truth. In the decade or so between abandoning my second first book and starting this one, I had grown engaged, enthralled, consumed with nonfiction, even though I wasn't, then or now, exactly certain what that meant. For me, the key, as in fiction, was *narrative*: We were telling stories, not transmitting facts. I had, by this time, spent a long while, a decade or more, working as a journalist and I understood (or thought I did) the limitations of this way of thought. That summer, as I gathered material for my *Weekly* piece, I cut two photos out of newspapers, one from the *Los Angeles Times* and the other from *The New York Times*. Both had appeared on the same morning, and both featured Bill and Hillary Clinton, on the dais of some event together, interacting in very different ways. This was the summer of the impeachment, or, as Philip Roth would acidly describe it, "the summer of an enormous piety binge, a purity binge, when terrorism — which had replaced communism as the prevailing threat to the country's security — was succeeded by cocksucking." In the image from the *Los Angeles Times*, the Clintons were scowling, backs turned and glaring off into the middle distance as if on opposite sides of an unbridgeable divide. In *The New York Times*, they were facing each other and smiling broadly, as if sharing a private joke. What stories were these pictures telling? Which was accurate . . . or (if this is even relevant) *true*? That is the conundrum stirred by nonfiction, the question raised whenever we sit down and try to craft a narrative out of the chaos of our experience, whether that narrative is personal, or reported, or some combination of the two.

Did I mention that my book was about earthquakes? Or that it was a book I hadn't necessarily meant to write? These are facts too, although what truths they reveal, I'm not sure I know. Earthquakes had been a fascination since before I came to California; I delayed moving west because I worried over living in a seismic zone. Eventually, I realized that a quake could hit while I was visiting just as easily as if I were a resident; what mattered was where you were standing when the shaking started, not where you made your home. It was random — or if not random, then expressive of a different order, one too vast, too sprawling, to be understood on our terms. Call it geologic as opposed to human time: That's how the seismologists described it, although I preferred to see it as a strategy, a way to read time, even deep time, not as an abstraction but as concrete. This, for me, had always been the issue — evanescence, loss, the ephemerality of everything. It had been a driving concern of my second first book, and I was unsurprised to see it re-emerge, albeit with a sharper focus, a newfound sense (if not quite acceptance) that the only possible response to anything was to remain present, to worry not about what might happen or what had already happened, but *what was happening now*. The idea, I recognized as I was writing, was that seismicity could root us, that in its unpredictable predictability, it offered an unlikely sort of faith. That was not what I had meant to write, but I'd learned by now to be responsive to the text — to give up, in other words, the desire for control that had waylaid me in those first two first books, the need to know from the outset what the point was, what the themes were, to tell the story from the top down rather than the bottom up.

The book scared the shit out of me; can I say that now? I didn't know how to write it, even how to start. I sold it off the piece in the *Weekly*, spent six months watching the deadline ticking ever closer while I wrote sporadically, if at all. I made a couple of research trips, went through my notes and interviews. I'd hoped the article might offer a starting point, but the more I considered it, the more I realized that I would have to disassemble everything I had written, everything I was thinking, that I would have to approach it all anew. Unlike my first two first books, this one was not inspired by envy but by opportunity: In writing the initial story, I had gathered so much material — so much *unused* material — that I'd had the fantasy the book would write itself. I knew how I wanted it to open, the lie of a misremembered earthquake, but after that, I had no idea of where to go. Then, one afternoon, returning from a visit to the United States Geological Survey field office in Pasadena, I had a moment when I saw the structure whole. I was on the 110, just north of downtown, and I remember pulling onto the shoulder so I could write it down. And yet, this can't be true; I drive that road now and can't imagine where I might have stopped, even though I still have the sheet of yellow legal paper breaking down the book, scrawl nearly illegible. The book would be written in nine chapters, a nod to the Richter Scale, and these would function as a palindrome, with a hinge in the middle, like a peak. There would be echoes, reflections; the first and last chapters would start in the same way. I see now that I was building a frame that would be both solid enough and flexible enough to enfold the elements I wanted: research, personal narrative, meditation, science, commentary. But in that instant, I had the sense that I was inventing a form, and what astonished me when I finished two years later was just how closely I had adhered to the plan.

Of course, opportunity is a double-edged sword, which I came to realize as I worked. The book did not write itself, even with my chapter notes, and I often felt as if I was pressing up against the edges of my competence, as if I had bitten off too much. "Every book," Annie Dillard has written, "has an intrinsic impossibility, which its writer discovers as soon as his first excitement dwindles. The problem . . . is insoluble . . . [a] prohibitive structural defect the writer wishes he had never noticed. He writes in spite of that." For me, this defect was not in the book but in myself. I was not smart enough, not adept enough, not a good enough writer or thinker to live up to my premise, which felt, at times, as if it had been bestowed on me by someone else. Here's Dillard again: "I do not so much write a book as sit up with it, as with a dying friend. During visiting hours, I enter its room with dread and sympathy for its many disorders. I hold its hand and hope it will get better." This had been the case with my first two first books, and it was the case with this one too. The difference was . . . what? That I was older? Under contract? Certainly, yes, this was part of it. But even more, in blundering through those projects, I had learned something about how expectations can derail us, that the only remedy for fear (or, let's be honest, ambition) is to sit down and work.

In the end, I wrote most of the book in a six-month push before my third deadline, the one my editor warned me not to miss. (What he said was: "The only way you should miss this deadline is if your car goes off a cliff and you are in it," an admonition I often repeat to myself.) It seemed as if I'd been working on it forever, which in a sense I had. First first book, second first book, third first book . . . all components of a process, growing one out of the other in a way I'm still not sure I can explain. I've never felt this raw, this out of my element, this drive to expiate my insufficiencies by completing not just a draft but a final manuscript. I've written other books, each of which a different story, fraught with its own frustrations, failures, fears. Yet in those initial moments — initial moments? initial months, initial years — after finishing *this* book, all I knew was the numbness of relief. *Thank God*, I thought. *That's done with. Now I never have to do it again.*

David L. Ulin is the author, most recently, of the novella *Labyrinth*. His other books include *The Lost Art of Reading: Why Books Matter in a Distracted Time* and *Writing Los Angeles: A Literary Anthology*, which received a 2002 California Book Award. He is book critic of the *Los Angeles Times*.

L.A. WRITERS' LAB BOOKS ON WRITING

---

writers tribe books

COMING FALL 2013 FROM
WRITERS TRIBE BOOKS

Two Small Birds by Dave Newman

Dan Charles reads Whitman the way some people read the Bible. He works three jobs. He attends college. Dan's older brother sells industrial parts and wants out. Dan wants something. In *Two Small Birds,* the brothers take flight in the worst possible way. This is the story of what it means to be family, to be working class, and to dream of being a poet in a world that refuses books. Set in tiny apartments and roadside diners, truckstops and warehouses, dive bars and worse hotels, *Two Small Birds* is a story of misdemeanors and perseverance, the jobs we take and the lives we lose. It's the story of love, and whoever is in charge of that.